THORSONS · GUIDE · TO
THE VERY BEST OF
Vegetarian
COOKING

Contributors of recipes to this book from their existing titles in *The Best of Vegetarian Cooking* series, Thorsons Publishers Ltd, are:

Desda Crockett (*Salads*)

Harvey Day (*Indian Curries*)

Rachael Holme (*Baking Better Breads*)

Janet Hunt (*Italian Dishes, Pasta Dishes, Pizzas and Pancakes, Quiches and Flans* and *Simple and Speedy Wholefood Cooking*)

Leon Lewis (*Vegetarian Dinner Parties*)

Jane O'Brien (*The Magic of Tofu*)

Craig and Ann Sams (*The Brown Rice Cookbook*)

THORSONS · GUIDE · TO
THE VERY BEST OF
Vegetarian
COOKING

Edited by Janet Hunt

Illustrated by Paul Turner

TREASURE PRESS

First published in Great Britain in 1984 by
Thorsons Publishers Limited

This edition published in 1987 by
Treasure Press
59 Grosvenor Street
London W1

© Thorsons Publishers Limited 1984

ISBN 1 85051 184 5

Printed in Czechoslovakia

50661

Contents

Introduction

It wasn't so long ago that vegetarians were regarded as an eccentric minority, and if not mocked then at least pitied for the way they must surely suffer when it came to mealtimes. Now, however, all that is changing. Vegetarians exist in such large numbers that they can no longer be dismissed as a minority, nor can they be ignored. Not just speciality shops and co-operatives, but supermarkets too now stock the ingredients they need. Restaurants know that an omelette will no longer do and — if they know their business — add at least a couple of meatless dishes to their menu. Even airlines cater for vegetarians, if given advance warning.

There are also many people who, though not completely vegetarian, enjoy meatless meals regularly for any of a variety of reasons. They may be concerned about their intake of saturated fats, or want to lose weight. Maybe the housekeeping budget won't stretch to expensive meat protein every day of the week. Or they may just enjoy the opportunity to be creative in the kitchen, to impress family and guests with something completely different.

No doubt about it, vegetarian cooking in the West has improved enormously. Fifty or so years ago a vegetarian cook had only a few basics, plus a limited supply of locally grown vegetables and fruit, from which to produce meal after meal. Today's cook may be spoiled for choice! Tofu, buckwheat noodles, miso, aubergines, kohlrabi, gomasio, tvp, agar-agar, avocado . . . the list is long, and growing. Add to these new cooking techniques, time- and energy-saving equipment, and recipes collected from around the world (many from countries where vegetarianism has long been part of the culture), and no-one has any excuse any more for producing boring food.

The popularity of wholefoods is also becoming widespread, and although vegetarianism and wholefoods are not necessarily synonymous, anyone interested in one is likely to be interested in the other. Once you have decided to eliminate or cut back on flesh foods, you'll need to replace them with others of equal — or preferably higher — nutritional value. Wholefoods fill this gap without making a great hole in the pocket whilst at the same time eliminating many of the risks now associated with refined foods.

The end result of these trends is a whole new attitude to cooking without meat, an attitude you'll find reflected in **The Very Best Of Vegetarian Cooking** It is based on the very popular **Best Of Vegetarian Cooking** series published by Thorsons Publishers Ltd, a selection of books devised to cater for all tastes, for those new to the kitchen as well as experienced cooks seeking new ideas, for errant carnivores and strict vegans. This compilation features many of the recipes you tell us you like best, presented in the same easy-to-follow format, with 24 colour plates to show you how attractive the dishes can look. It also includes a few recipes from outside the series, so even those who have collected the original books will find something new here.

Dip into them often. They will, hopefully, prove to you once and for all that giving up meat does not necessarily mean giving up the pleasure of preparing and eating good food.

Note: Most of the quantities given should be sufficient to satisfy 4 average appetites. Some of the quick and easy recipes are given in smaller quantities on the assumption that they might be used for a lunchtime snack by someone eating alone; a few of the more sumptuous dishes are given in larger amounts with dinner parties in mind. Where quantities do vary in this way, reference is made to the fact.

Glossary

Agar-Agar. Used by vegetarians in place of gelatine. It is made from seaweed and is highly nutritious. Buy flavoured or unflavoured from health food or wholefood stores.

Asafoetida. A popular curry spice, available from Indian food shops.

Bamboo Shoot Strips. A yellow, fibrous vegetable cut into strips and tinned in water. Used in Chinese cookery; buy it from speciality stores.

Beansprouts. Generally grown from mung beans, though other beans and grains will sprout successfully. Rich in vitamins B and C, also protein. Although they are widely available now, and inexpensive to buy, try growing your own at home so you always have some handy to throw into salads and other savouries.

Bulgur or **Burghul.** Made from wheat, this is a light and quick-to-cook grain. Inexpensive and widely available.

Butter. A natural and nutritious food, but very rich in fats. Use sparingly, although vegetarians need worry less about cholesterol as they have already eliminated meat, the main source of saturated fats in the average diet.

Carob. A chocolate-like powder to use in sweets and drinks. Caffeine-free and naturally sweet, it makes an excellent substitute for chocolate. Buy from health food or wholefood stores.

Cheeses. A protein-rich food ideal for vegetarians, but keep the very fatty varieties to a minimum. Many are made with rennet (the lining of a calf's stomach), though cheeses made with vegetable rennet are available widely nowadays. Soft cheeses are often made without rennet.

Dried Fruits. A good source of minerals (especially iron). Use as a sweetener instead of white sugar, or to replace sweets.

Eggs. Try to use free-range eggs whenever possible.

Flour. Wholemeal flour contains bran and wheatgerm, both of which are extracted during the production of white flour. It is also rich in natural fibre. Buy in small quantities and store somewhere cool and dry.

Garam Masala. A mixture of ground spices added to curried dishes, usually at the end of the cooking time. On sale in many outlets including supermarkets.

Ghee. Clarified butter used in Indian cooking. Buy it in tins from speciality stores. At a pinch you can use butter instead.

Grains. An underrated source of protein. Rice is probably the most popular grain — make sure you use brown rice. Others to try are millet, bulgur, buckwheat, barley, oats, corn, wholewheat berries, rye.

Herbs. These aid digestion and add interest to food. Best when fresh, but dried herbs make a good alternative.

Hoisin Sauce. A thick, dark sauce based on fermented soya beans, and used in Chinese cookery. Available in tins or glass jars from speciality shops.

Honey. Easily digested, rich in vitamins and minerals, and a useful alternative to white sugar. Buy the natural, unrefined kind.

Margarine. Use the softer varieties that are low in cholesterol, high in polyunsaturates (check the label).

Milk. A very concentrated liquid — it should be considered a food rather than a drink, and used sparingly in the adult diet. Low fat varieties are well worth considering, as is soya milk (see below).

Miso. A thick, strongly flavoured paste made from soya beans, and a good source of protein. Add at the last minute to soups, stews and casseroles.

Molasses. Best if unsulphured. A dark syrup that is high in minerals, contains an amazingly small amount of calories.

Nuts. A valuable source of protein in the vegetarian and vegan diet. Eat them frequently but sparingly as they are high in calories.

Oils. Unrefined oils are best, but rather expensive. Pure vegetable oils such as sunflower, safflower, olive, corn, sesame are all good choices.

Panch Phora. A mixture of seeds to use in curries. Buy it in packets at speciality stores and Indian food shops.

Pasta. Use wholemeal pasta which is now available in a variety of shapes and forms. You can also make your own pasta at home with little effort.

Pulses. This is the collective name for beans, peas and lentils. Pulses are an excellent source of protein, especially when combined with grains or dairy produce. Soya beans are most nutritious, but also take longest to cook. Buy them flaked to add to soups and casseroles, or in other forms such as soya grits, soya milk and tvp.

Soya Milk. High in protein but contains no animal fats, and so is low in saturates. It comes ready to be used, as a powder, or in concentrated form that you dilute with water. Vegans, or anyone wishing to reduce their intake of animal fats, can use soya milk to replace cow's milk in any recipe.

Sweet Brown Rice. This is an especially glutinous variety from Japan. Its texture makes it ideal for desserts. You should be able to find it in speciality shops.

Tahini. A paste made from sesame seeds. Now available through a variety of outlets, it comes in lighter and darker versions, both equally versatile and highly nutritious.

Tamari Soya Sauce. This is a naturally fermented soya sauce containing protein and vitamin B_{12}. It has an interesting and very distinctive salty flavour.

Tvp (Textured Vegetable Protein). Cheap, low in calories and cholesterol free, this easy-to-use and versatile food is made from the soya bean. It can now be bought not just in speciality stores, but also in most supermarkets.

Wakame. Like most seaweeds, wakame is rich in amino acids, trace elements and vitamins. Can be sautéed alone or with other vegetables, or added to stews and casseroles. Wakame and other seaweeds are available from speciality shops, and most health food and wholefood stores.

Wheatgerm. The heart of the wheat and very nutritious. Can be added to a variety of sweet and savoury dishes. Buy in small amounts and store in the cool.

Yogurt. Full of nutrients and especially easy to digest. Use the natural variety rather than those that have been over-flavoured and over-sweetened.

Family Favourites

Broad Bean Casserole

Imperial/Metric	American
1½ lb (680g) broad beans	1½ pounds Windsor beans
2 tablespoonsful vegetable oil	2 tablespoonsful vegetable oil
1 large green pepper	1 large green pepper
2 sticks celery	2 stalks celery
2 large carrots	2 large carrots
½ pint (285ml) vegetable stock (or water in which beans are cooked)	1⅓ cupsful vegetable stock (or water in which beans are cooked)
1-2 teaspoonsful mixed herbs	1-2 teaspoonsful mixed herbs
Seasoning to taste	Seasoning to taste
4 oz (115g) Cheddar cheese	1 cupful Cheddar cheese

1.   Cook the beans in lightly salted water until tender (or cook extra at a previous meal and keep in the fridge until needed).

2.   Meanwhile, heat the oil and gently sauté the finely chopped pepper, celery and carrots.

3.   When tender, mix with the drained broad beans (Windsor beans). Add the stock, herbs, seasoning, and 3 oz (85g) of grated cheese. Turn into a greased casserole.

4.   Bake at 400°F/200°C (Gas Mark 6) for 20 minutes. Remove from the heat, top with the remaining grated cheese and return to the oven for 5 more minutes.

Leek and Cheese Meringue

For pastry:

Imperial/Metric	American
3 oz (85g) polyunsaturated margarine	⅓ cupful polyunsaturated margarine
7 oz (200g) plain wholemeal flour	1¾ cupsful plain wholewheat flour
3 oz (85g) grated Cheddar cheese	¾ cupful grated Cheddar cheese
Approx. 4 tablespoonsful water	Approx. ⅓ cupful water
1-2 tablespoonsful caraway seeds	1-2 tablespoonsful caraway seeds

For filling:

Imperial/Metric	American
½ lb (225g) leeks	8 ounces leeks
1 tablespoonful vegetable oil	1 tablespoonful vegetable oil

For topping:

Imperial/Metric	American
2 egg whites	2 egg whites
Seasoning to taste	Seasoning to taste
2 oz (55g) grated Cheddar cheese	½ cupful grated Cheddar cheese

1.   To make the pastry, rub the margarine lightly into the flour, add the cheese, then enough water to bind to a dough.

2.   Sprinkle with the seeds, knead lightly, then wrap and leave in a cool place for at least 30 minutes.

3.   Roll out the pastry and line the flan dish; bake 'blind' at 375°F/190°C (Gas Mark 5) for 20 minutes.

4.   Meanwhile, clean and chop the leeks into 1 in. (2.5cm) segments, then sauté briefly in the oil; sprinkle with water, cover the pan, and cook gently until just tender.

5.   Make the meringue topping by whisking the egg whites and seasoning until stiff, then folding in the grated cheese.

6.   Arrange the drained leeks in the flan case; top with the meringue, and bake at 325°F/170°C (Gas Mark 3) for 20 minutes. Serve immediately.

Illustrated opposite page 16.

Potato and Walnut Loaf

Imperial/Metric	American
4 large cooked potatoes	4 large cooked potatoes
1 large green pepper	1 large green pepper
2 eggs	2 eggs
4 oz (115g) walnut pieces	1 cupful English walnut pieces
2 teaspoonsful mixed herbs	2 teaspoonsful mixed herbs
Seasoning to taste	Seasoning to taste
2 tablespoonsful wholemeal breadcrumbs	2 tablespoonsful wholewheat breadcrumbs
½ oz (15g) polyunsaturated margarine	1 tablespoonful polyunsaturated margarine

1. Mash the potatoes; chop the pepper finely; beat the eggs.

2. Combine all these with the nuts, herbs and seasoning, and transfer to a lightly greased loaf tin.

3. Top with the breadcrumbs and dot with margarine.

4. Bake at 350°F/180°C (Gas Mark 4) for 30 minutes.

Soyaburgers

Imperial/Metric	American
1 lb (455g) soya beans, cooked, drained and mashed	2 cupsful soy beans, cooked, drained and mashed
½ lb (225g) brown rice	1 cupful brown rice
1 onion, minced	1 onion, minced
1 small carrot, grated	1 small carrot, grated
4 oz (115g) wholemeal breadcrumbs	2 cupsful wholewheat breadcrumbs
2 tablespoonsful soya sauce	2 tablespoonsful soy sauce
1 egg *or*	1 egg *or*
¼ pint (140ml) soya milk	¾ cupful soy milk
2 oz (55g) wholemeal flour	½ cupful wholewheat flour
Seasoning to taste (e.g. herbs, garlic, *or* curry powder, cumin)	Seasoning to taste (e.g. herbs, garlic, *or* curry powder, cumin)
Vegetable oil for frying	Vegetable oil for frying

1. Combine all the ingredients together and knead the mixture for a couple of minutes to bind it.

2. Form the mixture into patties and deep-fry or shallow-fry them in the oil, turning them once.

Onion Crumble

For crumble:

Imperial/Metric	American
6 oz (170g) wholemeal flour	1½ cupsful wholewheat flour
3 oz (85g) polyunsaturated margarine *or* butter	⅓ cupful polyunsaturated margarine *or* butter
Good pinch of thyme	Good pinch of thyme

For base:

Imperial/Metric	American
1½ lbs (680g) onions	1½ pounds onions
3 tablespoonsful peanut butter	3 tablespoonsful peanut butter
1-2 teaspoonsful yeast extract	1-2 teaspoonsful yeast extract
Fresh thyme *or* parsley	Fresh thyme *or* parsley
Seasoning to taste	Seasoning to taste

1. To make the crumble, put the flour into a bowl and use your fingertips to rub in the fat, making a crumb-like mixture; stir in the thyme.

2. Peel and slice the onions, and steam or boil them in a little water for 10 minutes. Drain lightly, then stir in the peanut butter and yeast extract to taste, blending them well so that they dissolve to make a creamy sauce. Add a generous amount of chopped herbs and seasoning.

3. Spoon the mixture into an ovenproof dish and sprinkle with the crumble, pressing down gently to make an even topping.

4. Bake at 375°F/190°C (Gas Mark 5) for 20 minutes, or until the crumble is cooked. Serve hot garnished with more thyme or parsley.

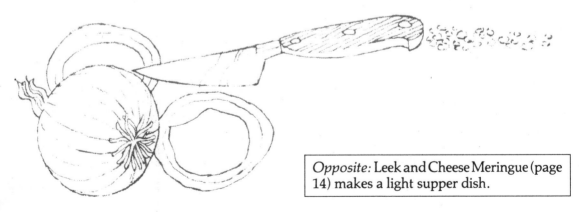

Opposite: Leek and Cheese Meringue (page 14) makes a light supper dish.

Jacket Potatoes

Imperial/Metric	*American*
2 small potatoes, *or* **1 large, for each person**	**2 small potatoes,** *or* **1 large, for each person**

1. Wash and dry the potatoes, prick with a fork and cook until just softening.

2. Make a cross in each potato and top with one of the following fillings:

- Cottage cheese and chives.
- Scrambled eggs and mushrooms.
- A spoonful of tahini and beansprouts.
- Baked beans.
- Fried onion and pepper with grated cheese.
- Soured cream and chopped onion.
- Sweetcorn and a knob of butter or polyunsaturated margarine.
- Leftover ratatouille.
- Fresh chopped herbs in yogurt.
- Any thick soup that is handy.
- Leftover curry sauce with nuts.

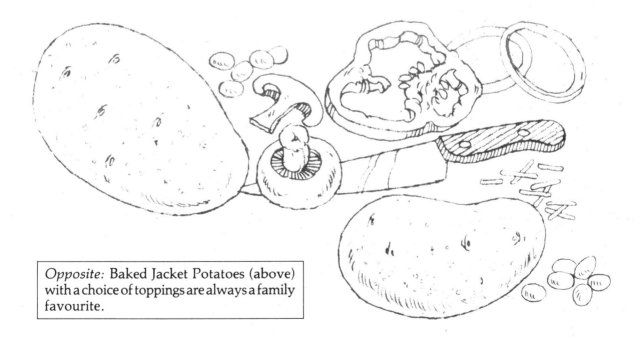

Opposite: Baked Jacket Potatoes (above) with a choice of toppings are always a family favourite.

Mixed Vegetable Curry

Imperial/Metric	American
1 tablespoonful ghee *or* vegetable fat	1 tablespoonful ghee *or* vegetable fat
4 onions, thinly sliced	4 onions, thinly sliced
4 cloves garlic, chopped	4 cloves garlic, chopped
1 green chilli, halved	1 green chilli, halved
3 or 4 curry leaves	3 or 4 curry leaves
4 × ½ in. (1cm) slivers green ginger	4 × ½ inch slivers green ginger
2 teaspoonsful garam masala	2 teaspoonsful garam masala
Seeds of 4 cardamoms	Seeds of 4 cardamoms
Seasonal vegetables	Seasonal vegetables
1¼ pints (710ml) vegetable stock (*or* Vecon, Marmite *or* Yeastrel stock)	3 cupsful vegetable stock (*or* Vecon, Marmite *or* Yeastrel stock)
¼ coconut, ground	¼ coconut, ground
Sea salt to taste	Sea salt to taste
2 teaspoonsful tamarind juice	2 teaspoonsful tamarind juice

1.   Heat the fat and fry the onions, garlic, green chilli, curry leaves and ginger for 2 minutes.

2.   Add the spices and fry for another 2 minutes.

3.   Chop or dice about 1-1½ lbs/455-680g (3-4 cupsful) of green peas, carrots, beans, cabbage, cauliflower or any other vegetables in season, using only a little of each kind.

4.   Cover the vegetables with the stock, adding a little water if necessary. Mix in the coconut and salt to taste.

5.   Boil the vegetables until tender, then stir in the tamarind juice a minute or two before serving.

Note: This curry should not be too watery. Remember that *Marmite, Yeastrel* and *Vecon* contain a great deal of salt, as does celery. (If you put a stick or two of celery through a juicer, you will be amazed how salty it tastes.)

Illustrated opposite page 113.

Sweetcorn Pancakes

For batter:

Imperial/Metric	American
3 oz (85g) buckwheat flour	¾ cupful buckwheat flour
2 oz (55g) plain wholemeal flour	½ cupful plain wholewheat flour
Pinch of sea salt	Pinch of sea salt
1 egg	1 egg
½ pint (285ml) water	1⅓ cupsful water

For filling:

Imperial/Metric	American
½ lb (225g) sweetcorn, fresh *or* frozen	1⅓ cupsful sweetcorn, fresh *or* frozen
1 small green pepper	1 small green pepper
1 small red pepper	1 small red pepper
2 oz (55g) cream cheese	¼ cupful cream cheese
2½ fl oz (70ml) plain yogurt	¼ cupful plain yogurt
Seasoning to taste	Seasoning to taste
3 medium tomatoes	3 medium tomatoes

1.   Sieve together the flours, add the salt, then stir in the egg.

2.   Gradually pour in the water, stirring continually, and beat well until you have a smooth, creamy batter. Leave in the fridge for at least 30 minutes, then beat again before using.

3.   Make up the pancakes, and keep them warm while you prepare the filling.

4.   Cook the sweetcorn with the finely chopped peppers, drain well, and mix in the cheese and yogurt until they melt to make a sauce. Season to taste.

5.   Use to fill pancakes and then top each one with a few slices of tomato.

Bean and Pasta Stew

Imperial/Metric	*American*
1 large carrot	1 large carrot
1 large onion	1 large onion
1 large leek	1 large leek
1 large potato	1 large potato
1 tablespoonful vegetable oil	1 tablespoonful vegetable oil
½ pint (285ml) water	1⅓ cupsful water
2 teaspoonsful mixed herbs	2 teaspoonsful mixed herbs
2 teaspoonsful tomato purée	2 teaspoonsful tomato paste
3 oz (85g) well cooked haricot beans (freshly prepared, leftovers *or* tinned)	½ cupful well cooked navy beans (freshly prepared, leftovers *or* canned)
3 oz (85g) wholemeal pasta shells	1½ cupsful wholewheat pasta shells
Seasoning to taste	Seasoning to taste

1.   Peel and slice the carrot and onion; chop the leek into ½ in. (1cm) sections; peel and cube the potato.

2.   Heat the vegetable oil in a pan and gently sauté the prepared vegetables for a few minutes.

3.   Add the water, herbs and tomato purée; bring to boil, then cover and simmer the vegetables for no more than 10 minutes.

4.   Add the beans and pasta and cook for 20 minutes longer, or until all the ingredients are just tender.

5.   Season to taste and serve.

Rissole Nut Mix

Imperial/Metric	American
4 oz (115g) ground walnuts	1 cupful ground English walnuts
4 oz (115g) wholemeal breadcrumbs	2 cupsful wholewheat breadcrumbs
1 onion, finely diced	1 onion, finely diced
Dash of freshly ground black pepper	Dash of freshly ground black pepper
2 eggs	2 eggs
1 teaspoonful *Marmite or Vecon*	1 teaspoonful *Marmite or Vecon*
6 tablespoonsful milk	½ cupful milk

1.   Mix together the nuts, breadcrumbs, onion and seasoning.

2.   Beat the eggs with the *Marmite* (or *Vecon*) and milk and then combine all the ingredients.

3.   Set the mixture aside for 30 minutes, then place it in a greased ovenproof dish and steam it for 2 hours, or bake it for 1 hour at 300°F/150°C (Gas Mark 2), standing the dish in water.

4.   Serve hot or cold or fried in slices.

Brussels Sprouts with Chestnuts

Imperial/Metric	American
1 lb (455g) Brussels sprouts	1 pound Brussels sprouts
¾ lb (340g) chestnuts	12 ounces chestnuts
1 oz (30g) polyunsaturated margarine *or* butter	2½ tablespoonsful polyunsaturated margarine *or* butter
1 pint (570ml) vegetable stock	2½ cupsful vegetable stock
Freshly ground black pepper	Freshly ground black pepper

1.   Wash and trim the sprouts and cook until tender.

2.   Split the shells of the chestnuts and boil them steadily for 5-10 minutes, then remove the shells and inner skins while still warm.

3.   Put the chestnuts in a saucepan with half the fat and the stock, cover and cook until soft.

4.   Meanwhile, gently sauté the sprouts in the rest of the fat, shaking the pan frequently. Add the pepper. Turn the chestnuts into the pan and mix them with the sprouts, and eat at once.

Illustrated between pages 96 and 97.

Scrambled Egg Flan

Imperial/Metric	American
Pastry to line an 8 in. (20cm) flan dish (see page 61)	Pastry to line an 8 inch flan dish (see page 61)
2 oz (55g) peas, fresh *or* frozen	⅓ cupful peas, fresh *or* frozen
1 oz (30g) polyunsaturated margarine	2½ tablespoonsful polyunsaturated margarine
1 small red pepper	1 small red pepper
2 oz (55g) mushrooms	1 cupful mushrooms
6 eggs	6 eggs
3 tablespoonsful cream *or* milk	3 tablespoonsful cream *or* milk
Seasoning to taste	Seasoning to taste
Parsley	Parsley

1.   Roll out the prepared pastry and line flan dish; bake blind at 400°F/200°C (Gas Mark 6) for 20-30 minutes, or until pastry is crisp and golden.

2.   Meanwhile, cook the peas in a little water. Drain well.

3.   Melt the margarine in a large pan and gently sauté the finely sliced pepper for 5 minutes; then add the chopped mushrooms and cook 5 minutes longer, stirring frequently.

4.   Beat the eggs together with the cream, season to taste, and add to the pan.

5.   Cook mixture on a low heat, stirring continually, until lightly set. Remove from heat immediately and then leave to cool in the pan for 2 or 3 minutes more.

6.   Stir in the hot peas.

7.   Spoon egg and vegetable scramble into the warm flan case, smooth the top, sprinkle with coarsely chopped fresh parsley. Serve at once.

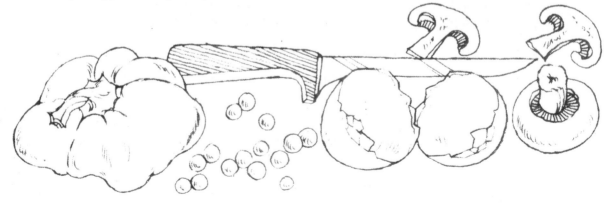

Stuffed Cabbage Leaves

Serves 6

Imperial/Metric	*American*
Approx. 12 cabbage leaves	Approx. 12 cabbage leaves
4 oz (115g) long-grain brown rice	½ cupful long-grain brown rice
1 medium onion, finely chopped	1 medium onion, finely chopped
2 cloves garlic, crushed	2 cloves garlic, crushed
4 tablespoonsful olive oil	4 tablespoonsful olive oil
1 teaspoonful oregano	1 teaspoonful oregano
1 teaspoonful dill	1 teaspoonful dill
Juice of 1 lemon	Juice of 1 lemon
1 tablespoonful tomato purée	1 tablespoonful tomato paste
1 tablespoonful almonds, blanched	1 tablespoonful almonds, blanched
1 tablespoonful Parmesan, finely grated	1 tablespoonful Parmesan, finely grated

1. Carefully strip the leaves from the cabbage and wash them. The outer leaves are more suitable for stuffing and there is no shortage of uses for the crisp heart of the cabbage.

2. Blanch the cabbage leaves to make them pliable by dropping them into boiling water for 2 minutes.

3. Cook the rice in boiling water for about 30 minutes, until it is tender and then drain it.

4. Fry the onion and garlic in 2 tablespoonsful of the oil for 1 minute.

5. Add the rice and the other ingredients. Continue to cook for 5 minutes on a low heat, stirring frequently.

6. Allow the filling to cool before stuffing the cabbage leaves. First, use a pair of scissors to cut out a section of the tough leaf stem. Put a level tablespoonful of the filling on the leaf at the top of your cut. Fold the leaf to the centre before tucking in the sides. Then roll up the leaf making a neat, tight package.

7. Pack the cabbage leaves tightly into a casserole, pour over them 2 tablespoonsful of olive oil, and bake at 350°F/180°C (Gas Mark 4) for about 40 minutes, or until tender.

Illustrated opposite page 48.

Nut Savoury Filled Ravioli

Imperial/Metric	American
½ lb (225g) basic pasta dough (see below)	8 ounces basic pasta dough (see below)
1 leek	1 leek
1 tablespoonful vegetable oil	1 tablespoonful vegetable oil
4 oz (115g) Brazil nuts, ground *or* finely chopped	¾ cupful Brazil nuts, ground *or* finely chopped
3 oz (85g) wholemeal breadcrumbs	1½ cupsful wholewheat breadcrumbs
1 oz (30g) wheatgerm	¼ cupful wheatgerm
1 teaspoonful sage, *or* to taste	1 teaspoonful sage, *or* to taste
Seasoning to taste	Seasoning to taste
Yeast extract (optional)	Yeast extract (optional)
1 oz (30g) melted polyunsaturated margarine	2½ tablespoonsful melted polyunsaturated margarine

1.   Roll out the pasta dough; cut into small squares; arrange half of them on a flat surface and put the rest aside.

2.   Fry the cleaned and finely chopped leek in the oil until soft; remove the pan from the heat and stir in the nuts, breadcrumbs, wheatgerm, sage and seasoning.

3.   Flavour the mixture with a little yeast extract if liked, then use a wooden spoon to mash all the ingredients and make a paste.

4.   Drop a small amount of the mixture in the centre of each of the squares of dough.

5.   Cover each one with another square of dough; dampen the edges and press firmly together.

6.   Bring salted water to the boil in a large pan and drop in the ravioli, a few at a time; cook gently for 5-10 minutes, or until they rise to the surface.

7.   Use a perforated spoon to remove the ravioli from the water; drain and serve with a little melted margarine trickled over them.

For pasta dough:

Imperial/Metric	American
½ lb (225g) wholemeal flour	2 cupsful wholewheat flour
Pinch of sea salt	Pinch of sea salt
1 large egg	1 large egg
Water to mix	Water to mix

1.   In a bowl sieve together the flour and salt.

2.   Make a well in the centre and pour in the lightly beaten egg; add just enough water to bind the ingredients and make a firm dough.

3.   On a floured board knead the dough until smooth and elastic. Allow to stand for a short time then proceed as above.

Note: This basic dough can also be used to make cannelloni, tagliatelle, lasagne and noodles. It is important to roll it out as thinly as possible.

Chick Pea Salad

Imperial/Metric	*American*
6 oz (170g) dried chick peas	¾ cupful dried garbanzo beans
1 small onion	1 small onion
½ small clove garlic	½ small clove garlic
Juice of 1 lemon	Juice of 1 lemon
3 dessertspoonsful olive oil	6 teaspoonsful olive oil
½ teaspoonful sea salt	½ teaspoonful sea salt
Cayenne pepper	Cayenne pepper
3 tablespoonsful finely chopped parsley	3 tablespoonsful finely chopped parsley

1.   Soak the chick peas overnight in enough cold water to cover them. In the morning, drain the peas and put them in a saucepan covered with cold water. Simmer the peas for about 1½ hours, topping up with more cold water when necessary. Drain them and allow to cool.

2.   Peel and chop the onion and garlic finely.

3.   Mix together the lemon juice, olive oil, garlic, salt and cayenne pepper.

4.   Put the peas and the chopped onion into a bowl, pour the dressing over, and mix thoroughly. Chill well before serving, garnished with parsley.

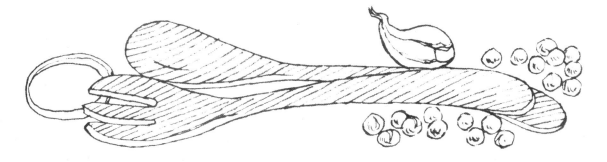

Italian Style Meatless Meatballs

Serves 6

Imperial/Metric	American
1 lb (455g) tofu, well broken up	2 cupsful tofu, well broken up
1 teaspoonful oregano	1 teaspoonful oregano
½ teaspoonful basil	½ teaspoonful basil
1 small onion, finely chopped	1 small onion, finely chopped
1 tablespoonful soya sauce (or to taste)	1 tablespoonful soy sauce (or to taste)

Plus either:

Imperial/Metric	American
2 eggs, lightly beaten and	2 eggs, lightly beaten and
1 oz (30g) wholemeal breadcrumbs	½ cupful wholewheat breadcrumbs

or:

Imperial/Metric	American
4 oz (115g) wholemeal flour and	1 cupful wholewheat flour and
2 oz (55g) wholemeal breadcrumbs	1 cupful wholewheat breadcrumbs

1.   Combine the ingredients well in a large bowl, kneading the mixture to help it hold together.

2.   Shape the mixture into balls and shallow-fry them. Then arrange in an ovenproof dish and cover with Spaghetti Sauce (see opposite).

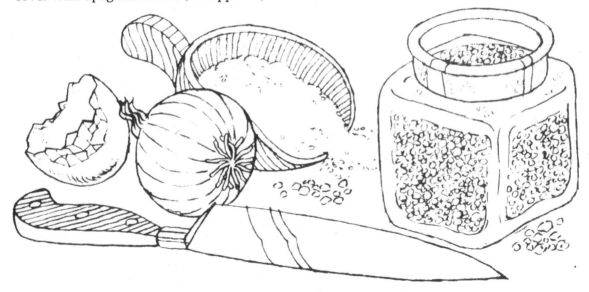

Spaghetti Sauce

Imperial/Metric	*American*
1 large onion, chopped	1 large onion, chopped
4 cloves garlic, minced	4 cloves garlic, minced
2 tablespoonsful vegetable oil	2 tablespoonsful vegetable oil
1 lb (455g) tofu, mashed well with a fork *or* leftover scrambled tofu	2 cupsful tofu, mashed well with a fork *or* leftover scrambled tofu
2 medium-sized tins tomatoes *or* 2 lb (900g) fresh tomatoes	2 medium-sized cans tomatoes *or* 2 pounds fresh tomatoes
1 small tin tomato purée	1 small can tomato paste
½ tablespoonful oregano	½ tablespoonful oregano
½ tablespoonful basil	½ tablespoonful basil
½ tablespoonful thyme	½ tablespoonful thyme
2 oz (55g) mushrooms, sliced	1 cupful mushrooms, sliced
Soya sauce to taste	Soy sauce to taste

1.   Sauté the onion and garlic in the oil and then add the other ingredients.

2.   Bring the mixture to the boil, reduce the heat and simmer the sauce for about 30 minutes.

Sweetcorn Fritters

Imperial/Metric	*American*
2 oz (55g) plain wholemeal flour	½ cupful plain wholewheat flour
Seasoning to taste	Seasoning to taste
¼ pint (140ml) milk	⅔ cupful milk
1 egg	1 egg
10 oz (285g) tin sweetcorn *or* frozen equivalent	10 ounce can sweetcorn *or* frozen equivalent
Vegetable oil for frying	Vegetable oil for frying

1.   Put the flour, seasoning, milk and egg into a bowl and beat until well blended.

2.   Add drained sweetcorn, and mix evenly through the batter.

3.   Gently fry spoonsful of the mixture in hot oil, turning once, for about 5 minutes or until fritters are a golden brown. Drain well, and serve hot with a protein-rich sauce.

Yorkshire Pudding with Vegetables

Imperial/Metric	American
4 large tomatoes	4 large tomatoes
6 oz (170g) button mushrooms	3 cupsful button mushrooms
1 oz (30g) polyunsaturated margarine	2½ tablespoonsful polyunsaturated margarine

For batter:

Imperial/Metric	American
4 oz (115g) wholemeal flour	1 cupful wholewheat flour
Sea salt	Sea salt
1 egg	1 egg
½ pint (285ml) milk *or* milk and water	1⅓ cupsful milk *or* milk and water

1.   Halve the tomatoes; wipe clean the mushrooms. In the oven, melt the margarine in a medium-sized tin, leaving it long enough for the tin to warm up. Arrange the vegetables evenly across the base of the tin.

2.   Sieve the flour and salt into a bowl. Add the egg.

3.   Gradually add the milk, stirring carefully with a wooden spoon to remove lumps, then beat or whisk to add air to the mixture. The batter can be used at once, but will give better results if left to stand in a cold place for a short time first.

4.   Spoon the batter over the vegetables. Bake at 450°F/230°C (Gas Mark 8) for about 10 minutes, or until beginning to rise. Lower the heat to 375°F/190°C (Gas Mark 5) and cook for 30 minutes, or until golden and cooked through. Serve cut into squares. A cheese, white or tomato sauce goes well with this dish.

Note: If preferred you can cook your Yorkshire pudding in small individual patty tins, in which case they will take about half the time.

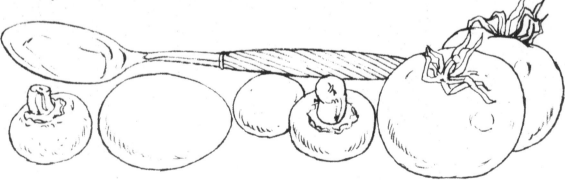

Aubergine Galette

For 6

Imperial/Metric	American
1 lb (455g) aubergines	1 pound eggplants
Sea salt	Sea salt
Approx. ¼ pint (140ml) olive oil	⅔ cupful olive oil
1 medium onion, finely chopped	1 medium onion, finely chopped
1 clove garlic, crushed	1 clove garlic, crushed
14 oz (395g) tin tomatoes	1 medium can tomatoes
¼ pint (140ml) yogurt	⅔ cupful yogurt

1.   Slice the aubergine (eggplant) into ½ in. (1cm) slices and sprinkle with sea salt. Leave for 30 minutes.

2.   Rinse and dry the aubergine slices.

3.   Heat the oil and fry the aubergines until brown.

4.   Fry the onions and garlic in some olive oil. After a few minutes, add the tomatoes (but not the juice).

5.   In a round, deep ovenproof dish, place alternate layers of aubergines, tomatoes and onions and yogurt.

6.   Leave for a day and then bake in a moderate oven at 350°F/180°C (Gas Mark 4) for 45 minutes.

7.   Allow to cool before turning out. A suitable garnish would be fresh herbs.

Note: If you turn the galette out too soon before the meal, it may spread, so it is recommended that you turn it out just before serving.

Macaroni Burgers

Imperial/Metric	American
4 oz (115g) wholemeal macaroni	2 cupsful wholewheat macaroni
2 oz (55g) polyunsaturated margarine	¼ cupful polyunsaturated margarine
2 oz (55g) plain wholemeal flour	½ cupful plain wholewheat flour
½ pint (285ml) milk	1⅓ cupsful milk
4 oz (115g) Cheddar cheese	1 cupful Cheddar cheese
2 oz (55g) cooked peas *or* green beans	⅓ cupful cooked peas *or* green beans
1 teaspoonful rosemary	1 teaspoonful rosemary
Approx. 2 oz (55g) wheatgerm	Approx. ½ cupful wheatgerm
Seasoning to taste	Seasoning to taste
Extra wheatgerm *or* wholemeal breadcrumbs	Extra wheatgerm *or* wholewheat breadcrumbs
Vegetable oil for frying	Vegetable oil for frying

1. Cook the macaroni until just tender; drain, and rinse through thoroughly with cold water; set aside.

2. Melt the margarine in a pan and lightly sauté the flour.

3. Remove from the heat; pour on the milk; return to the heat, and continue cooking and stirring until the sauce thickens.

4. Add the grated cheese, coarsely chopped peas or beans and crumbled rosemary. Season generously.

5. Mix the sauce with the drained macaroni and leave to cool.

6. Shape the mixture into burgers — if it is too soft, add a little wheatgerm or breadcrumbs.

7. Coat each one with wheatgerm and shallow-fry or deep-fry until crisp and golden.

Illustrated opposite page 32.

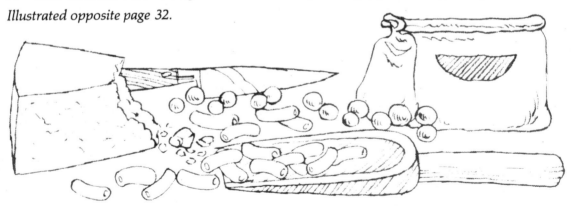

Baked Eggs on a Rice Bed

Serves 6

Imperial/Metric   *American*

1 onion, chopped	1 onion, chopped
Vegetable oil	Vegetable oil
¾ lb (340g) long-grain brown rice	1½ cupsful long-grain brown rice
Sea salt	Sea salt
Soya sauce	Soy sauce
6 eggs	6 eggs
Freshly ground black pepper	Freshly ground black pepper
6 oz (170g) grated, sharp cheese (e.g. mature Cheddar)	1½ cupsful grated, sharp cheese (e.g. mature Cheddar)
2 tablespoonsful wholemeal breadcrumbs	2 tablespoonsful wholewheat breadcrumbs

1.   Sauté the onion in oil until soft, then add the rice and stir-fry for another 3 minutes.

2.   Cover with ¾-1 pint/425-570ml (2-2½ cupsful) of boiling water, add salt or soya sauce to taste, and simmer until the water is absorbed (35-40 minutes).

3.   Oil a casserole dish and fill with cooked rice mixture.

4.   Break the eggs over the bed of rice — the yolks will probably break but this is not important.

5.   Sprinkle with the salt and pepper, then sprinkle with the grated cheese and finally add a thin layer of breadcrumbs.

6.   Bake for 20-25 minutes at 250°F/130°C (Gas Mark ½). Serve immediately sprinkled with chopped parsley.

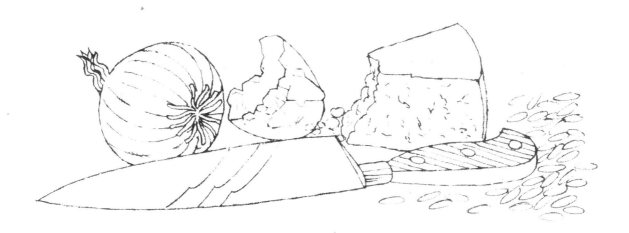

Leek Paella

Imperial/Metric	American
½ lb (225g) leeks	8 ounces leeks
2 oz (55g) polyunsaturated margarine	¼ cupful polyunsaturated margarine
6 oz (170g) brown rice	¾ cupful brown rice
1 pint (570ml) vegetable stock *or* water	2½ cupsful vegetable stock *or* water
4 medium tomatoes	4 medium tomatoes
Seasoning to taste	Seasoning to taste
2 tablespoonsful tahini *or* 2 oz (55g) toasted, flaked almonds	2 tablespoonsful tahini *or* ½ cupful toasted, slivered almonds

1.   Remove the outer and wilted leaves of the leeks, cut off the base. Cut into sections about 1 in. (2.5cm) long.

2.   Melt the margarine, add the leeks and cook gently for 3 minutes, stirring occasionally.

3.   Add the rice and fry for a few minutes longer.

4.   Stir in the liquid, quartered tomatoes and seasoning. Bring to the boil, cover and simmer until the rice is cooked (approximately 30 minutes).

5.   If using tahini, stir it in before serving the rice. Nuts can be sprinkled on top of individual portions.

Opposite: Macaroni Burgers (page 30) — wholefood fast food!

Quick and Easy

Shallow-Fried Tofu Steaks

Imperial/Metric	American
1 lb (450g) Tofu, sliced about ⅓ in. (8mm) thick	1 pound Tofu, sliced about ⅓ inch thick
Soya sauce	Soy sauce
Wholemeal flour (optional)	Wholewheat flour (optional)
Vegetable oil	Vegetable oil

1.   Leave the tofu slices in the soya sauce for a couple of minutes, then turn them and leave them again for another couple of minutes.

2.   Dip them in the flour; this will give a crispy coating.

3.   Fry the pieces of tofu in the oil for a few minutes on each side until they are nicely browned. Serve with vegetables and a salad.

Opposite: Meal-in-a-Soup (page 36) and Sweetcorn, Bean and Barley Soup (page 106) are ideal lunch or supper meals when served with wholemeal bread.

Miso Soup with Tofu Cubes

Imperial/Metric	American
A little vegetable oil	A little vegetable oil
1 onion, chopped	1 onion, chopped
1 carrot, sliced	1 carrot, sliced
1 stick celery, sliced	1 stalk celery, sliced
2 pints (1 litre) water	5 cupsful water
1 piece seaweed (wakame), rinsed and soaked for about 10 minutes, and finely chopped	1 piece seaweed (wakame), rinsed and soaked for about 10 minutes, and finely chopped
½ lb (225g) tofu, pressed until firm and cut into cubes	1 cupful tofu, pressed until firm and cut into cubes
1 tablespoonful miso *or* to taste	1 tablespoonful miso *or* to taste

1. Brush a little oil onto the base of a large pan and sauté the onion for a couple of minutes.

2. Add the carrot and celery and sauté them for a few minutes more.

3. Add the water and wakame, bring the soup to the boil and cook until the vegetables are done — about 20 minutes or so.

4. At the end of cooking, add the tofu cubes, bring the soup back to the boil briefly, then remove the pan from the heat and mix the miso with a small amount of soup stock to dissolve it.

5. Add this to the soup or put the miso into individual bowls and ladle the soup into the bowls; this way amounts of miso can be adjusted to each person's taste.

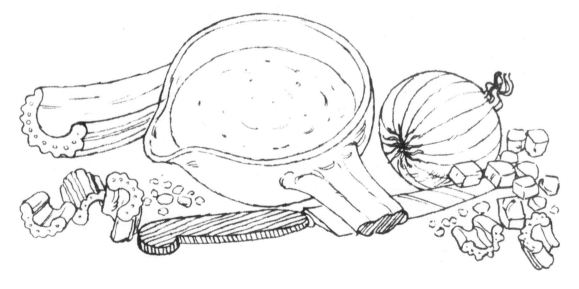

Parsnip Soup with Walnuts

Imperial/Metric	American
1 lb (455g) parsnips	1 lb parsnips
2 onions	2 onions
2 carrots	2 carrots
1 oz (30g) polyunsaturated margarine *or* butter	2½ tablespoonsful polyunsaturated margarine *or* butter
1 pint (570ml) vegetable stock	2½ cupsful vegetable stock
½ pint (285ml) milk	1⅓ cupsful milk
2 tablespoonsful single cream *or* natural yogurt	2 tablespoonsful single cream *or* natural yogurt
1 oz (30g) walnuts, chopped	¼ cupful chopped English walnuts
Seasoning to taste	Seasoning to taste

1. Peel the vegetables and chop them into small pieces.

2. Sauté them briefly in the melted margarine before adding them to the vegetable stock and milk, and bringing to the boil.

3. Cover and simmer for 30 minutes or until tender.

4. Purée the vegetables in a blender or press them through a sieve.

5. Return the purée to the saucepan and stir in the cream or yogurt, then heat the soup through very gently — it must not be allowed to boil.

6. Sprinkle with the walnuts just before eating.

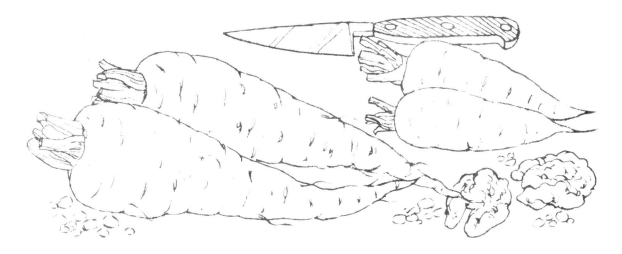

Meal-in-a-Soup

Imperial/Metric	American
½ oz (15g) polyunsaturated margarine	1 tablespoonful polyunsaturated margarine
1 small onion, sliced	1 small onion, sliced
1 oz (30g) red lentils, washed	2½ tablespoonsful red lentils, washed
1 stick celery, chopped	1 stalk celery, chopped
1 large tomato, chopped	1 large tomato, chopped
1 large carrot, chopped	1 large carrot, chopped
½ small green pepp r, chopped	½ small green pepper, chopped
¼ small cabbage, chopped	¼ small cabbage, chopped
1 pint (570ml) water	2½ cupsful water
1 teaspoonful yeast extract	1 teaspoonful yeast extract
Seasoning to taste	Seasoning to taste
1-2 oz (30-55g) grated cheese (optional)	¼-½ cupful grated cheese (optional)

1. Melt the margarine, then gently fry the onion until just changing colour.

2. Add the lentils, vegetables and water to the frying pan.

3. When boiling, stir in the yeast extract, season and leave to simmer for about 30 minutes. Although this soup is already a complete meal, you can boost the protein by topping it with grated cheese just before serving.

Note: The vegetables can also be varied according to what is in season. Mushrooms, courgettes (zucchini) and cauliflower taste especially good. This is meant to be a thick, hearty soup, but if necessary you can make it lighter by adding more water or vegetable stock.

Illustrated opposite page 33.

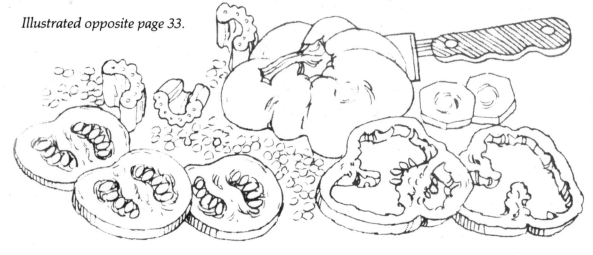

Spinach Egg Soup with Beansprouts

Imperial/Metric	American
2 pints (1 litre) vegetable stock	5 cupsful vegetable stock
2 eggs	2 eggs
½ teaspoonful cornflour	½ teaspoonful cornstarch
½ lb (225g) young spinach	8 ounces young spinach
4 tablespoonsful fresh beansprouts	⅓ cupful fresh beansprouts
Soya sauce	Soy sauce

1. Heat the stock to boiling point; beat the eggs with the cornflour (cornstarch).

2. Slowly pour the eggs through a sieve into the boiling stock; lower the heat and simmer for 1 or 2 minutes.

3. Add the washed, shredded spinach and beansprouts and cook for just 1 or 2 minutes more.

4. Serve at once with a little soya sauce added.

Rice Soup

Serves 6

Imperial/Metric	American
½ lb (225g) chopped onions	1¼ cupsful chopped onions
10 oz (285g) brown rice	1¼ cupsful brown rice
Pinch each of thyme, marjoram and sea salt	Pinch each of thyme, marjoram and sea salt
1 bay leaf	1 bay leaf
Vegetable oil	Vegetable oil
4 pints (2 litres) boiling water	10 cupsful boiling water
1 tablespoonful soya sauce	1 tablespoonful soy sauce
½ lb (225g) chick peas *or* haricot beans, pre-cooked	1¼ cupsful garbanzo beans *or* navy beans, pre-cooked

1. Sauté the first six ingredients in the oil until onions are transparent.

2. Add boiling water and pressure cook for 30 minutes. Push through a strainer.

3. Add tamari and chick peas (garbanzo beans) or haricot beans (navy beans). Re-heat gently before serving.

Beansprout Fritters

Imperial/Metric	American
1 large onion	1 large onion
2 oz (55g) mung beansprouts	1 cupful mung beansprouts
2 oz (55g) wholemeal breadcrumbs	1 cupful wholewheat breadcrumbs
1 tablespoonful vegetable oil	1 tablespoonful vegetable oil
½ teaspoonful herbs	½ teaspoonful herbs
Soya sauce	Soy sauce
Seasoning to taste	Seasoning to taste

1.   Chop the onion finely.

2.   Combine all the ingredients together well, using enough soya sauce to make the mixture stick together. If you need to use a good amount, you won't need to add salt.

3.   Shape into fritters and shallow-fry on both sides.

Cheese Waffles

Imperial/Metric	American
4 oz (115g) polyunsaturated margarine	½ cupful polyunsaturated margarine
½ lb (225g) plain wholemeal flour	2 cupsful plain wholewheat flour
½ pint (285ml) milk	1⅓ cupsful milk
2 eggs	2 eggs
1 teaspoonful herbs	1 teaspoonful herbs
6 oz (170g) Cheddar cheese	1½ cupsful Cheddar cheese

1.   Soften the margarine, put it into a bowl with the flour, milk, eggs and herbs; blend very thoroughly.

2.   The mixture should be thick and creamy; add more milk or water if it is too dry.

3.   Finely grate the cheese and stir it into the rest of the ingredients.

4.   Heat and oil the waffle iron; pour in the batter to fill two-thirds of the iron; close firmly and cook in the usual way.

Zen Hash

Serves 6

This dish was featured on the menu of the Zen Hashery, one of New York's earliest macrobiotic restaurants.

Imperial/Metric	American
2 lb (900g) courgettes	2 pounds zucchini
1 lb (455g) spinach	1 pound spinach
1 large onion	1 large onion
1 carrot	1 carrot
4 tablespoonsful vegetable oil	4 tablespoonsful vegetable oil
4 fl oz (120ml) soya sauce	½ cupful soy sauce
2 oz (55g) pine kernels *or* cashew nuts	½ cupful pine kernels *or* cashew nuts
Cooked brown rice	Cooked brown rice

1. Quarter and slice courgettes (zucchini).

2. Coarsely chop spinach and onion and grate carrot.

3. In a large frying pan (skillet), sauté onion until golden in colour.

4. Add courgettes (zucchini) and sauté until nearly done (about 5 minutes).

5. Add soya sauce and nuts and mix well, then add carrot and spinach and cook for another 3-5 minutes until spinach is done. Season to taste.

6. Place brown rice on plates with hollowed out beds in the middle to fill with the vegetable mixture.

7. Garnish with parsley sprigs, carrot sticks or whole radishes (including tops).

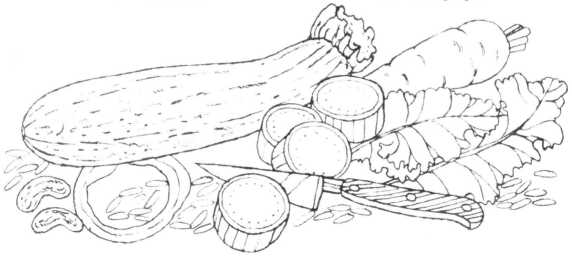

Mushrooms in Soured Cream

Serves 6

Imperial/Metric	American
2 medium onions, finely chopped	2 medium onions, finely chopped
3 oz (85g) butter	7½ tablespoonsful butter
2 lb (900g) mushrooms	2 pounds mushrooms
Sea salt and black pepper to taste	Sea salt and black pepper to taste
2 tablespoonsful wholemeal flour	2 tablespoonsful wholewheat flour
½ pint (285ml) soured cream	1⅓ cupsful soured cream
½ teaspoonful dill	½ teaspoonful dill
Parsley	Parsley

1. Fry the onion in the butter until transparent.

2. Add the mushrooms (leave button mushrooms whole and halve larger ones).

3. Add sea salt and freshly ground black pepper and cook gently for about 15 minutes.

4. Stir in the flour and add the soured cream gradually, followed by the dill.

5. Heat gently until the mushrooms are cooked.

6. Garnish with parsley.

Leeks Provencal

Serves 1

Imperial/Metric	American
2 leeks	2 leeks
2 tablespoonsful vegetable oil	2 tablespoonsful vegetable oil
2 tomatoes *or* tinned equivalent	2 tomatoes *or* canned equivalent
Squeeze of lemon juice	Squeeze of lemon juice
Seasoning to taste	Seasoning to taste
1 egg	1 egg

1. Wash and chop the leeks into small pieces.

2. Cook them gently in the oil for a few minutes, turning them occasionally and then add the chopped tomatoes, lemon juice and seasoning.

3. Simmer the mixture for 5 minutes and, meanwhile, boil the egg lightly.

4. When the leeks are ready, pour them onto a plate and top with the sliced egg.

Quick Yogurt Quiche

For base:

Imperial/Metric	American
6 oz (170g) wholemeal crackers *or* crispbread	6 ounces wholewheat crackers *or* crispbread
4 oz (115g) polyunsaturated margarine	½ cupful polyunsaturated margarine

For topping:

Imperial/Metric	American
3 eggs	3 eggs
1 small carton plain yogurt	1 small carton plain yogurt
¼ pint (140ml) milk *or* cream	⅔ cupful milk *or* cream
Seasoning to taste	Seasoning to taste
3 oz (85g) Cheddar cheese	¾ cupful Cheddar cheese
½ small cucumber	½ small cucumber
Chives	Chives

1. Crush the crackers and combine well with the melted margarine, then press the mixture firmly into the base of an 8 in. (20cm) flan dish.

2. Whisk the eggs, add the yogurt and milk; season well.

3. Grate the cheese and stir it into the mixture.

4. Slice the cucumber and layer it across the base of the prepared flan; pour in the liquid mixture; top with chopped chives.

5. Bake at 350°F/180°C (Gas Mark 4) for about 30 minutes, or until filling is set. Serve hot or cold.

Illustrated opposite page 160.

Cabbage Pancakes

Imperial/Metric	American
½ small green cabbage	½ small green cabbage
1 medium red pepper	1 medium red pepper
2 oz (55g) polyunsaturated margarine	¼ cupful polyunsaturated margarine
½ pint (285ml) milk and water mixed	1⅓ cupsful milk and water mixed
4 oz (115g) wholemeal flour	1 cupful wholewheat flour
1 egg	1 egg
Seasoning to taste	Seasoning to taste
Vegetable oil for frying	Vegetable oil for frying
Tahini, peanut butter *or* curd cheese	Tahini, peanut butter *or* curd cheese

1.   Fry the finely chopped cabbage and pepper in the margarine for 5 minutes, taking care they don't burn. Remove them from the pan.

2.   Make a pancake batter by mixing a little of the liquid with the flour and egg. Gradually add the rest of the liquid and beat until smooth. Season.

3.   Spoon the vegetables into the batter and combine well.

4.   Heat a little oil in a large pan and add a few spoonsful of the mixture. Shake gently to spread the mixture across the pan and cook until set underneath.

5.   Flip over and cook on the other side. Use up the rest of the batter in the same way.

6.   Serve each pancake topped with a spoonful of tahini, peanut butter or curd cheese.

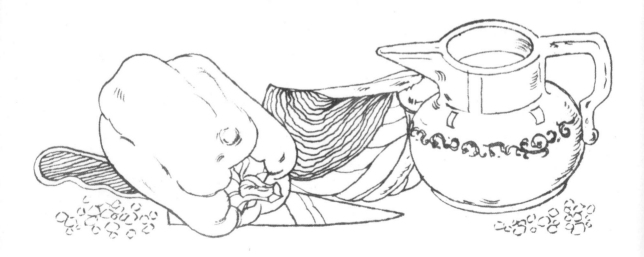

Macaroni and Vegetable Stew

Imperial/Metric	American
1 parsnip	1 parsnip
1 potato	1 potato
1 carrot	1 carrot
1 onion	1 onion
1 large leek	1 large leek
2 oz (55g) polyunsaturated margarine	¼ cupful polyunsaturated margarine
½ pint (285ml) vegetable stock	1⅓ cupsful vegetable stock
Soya sauce	Soy sauce
1-2 teaspoonsful mixed herbs	1-2 teaspoonsful mixed herbs
Seasoning to taste	Seasoning to taste
4 oz (115g) wholemeal macaroni	1½-2 cupsful wholewheat macaroni
Watercress to garnish	Watercress to garnish

1.   Peel and cube the parsnip, potato and carrot; slice the onion and leek.

2.   Melt the margarine and gently sauté the vegetables for a few minutes and add the stock. Season with soya sauce, herbs, sea salt and freshly ground black pepper.

3.   Simmer until the vegetables are cooked but still hold their shape.

4.   Meanwhile, cook the macaroni in boiling water.

5.   Combine the drained macaroni with the vegetables and stock, and heat for 2 minutes. Serve garnished with watercress.

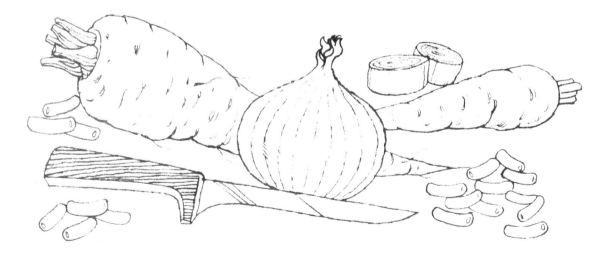

Cooked-in-the-Pan Pizza Margherita

For base:

Imperial/Metric	American
6 oz (170g) plain wholemeal flour	1½ cupsful plain wholewheat flour
1 good teaspoonful baking powder	1 good teaspoonful baking powder
Sea salt to taste	Sea salt to taste
Water to mix	Water to mix

For topping:

Imperial/Metric	American
4 medium tomatoes	4 medium tomatoes
6 oz (170g) Bel Paese cheese	1½ cupsful Bel Paese cheese
2 teaspoonsful oregano	2 teaspoonsful oregano
Approx. 1 tablespoonful vegetable oil	Approx. 1 tablespoonful vegetable oil
Seasoning to taste	Seasoning to taste
Vegetable oil for frying	Vegetable oil for frying

1. Mix together the flour, baking powder and salt in a bowl.

2. Add water gradually, kneading to make a dough.

3. Continue kneading until dough is smooth and soft, then divide into two, and roll out into thin rounds.

4. Pour a little oil into a heavy pan and heat until hot but not smoking, then turn down heat and cook pizza slowly for 2 minutes.

5. Turn the pizza and cover with 2 of the tomatoes, sliced thin, then half the cheese. Sprinkle with herbs and season well. Continue cooking for a few minutes to brown the underside of the pizza and heat the topping.

6. Put under the grill to melt the cheese. Meanwhile, cook the second pizza in the same way.

7. Serve cut into slices.

Illustrated opposite page 96.

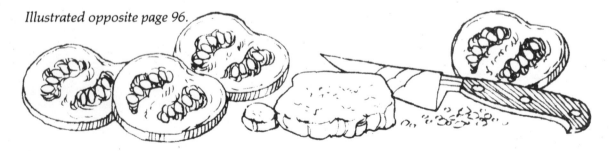

Colcannon

Serves 6

Imperial/Metric	American
3 oz (85g) butter	7½ tablespoonsful butter
1 medium onion, finely chopped	1 medium onion, finely chopped
½ cabbage, coarsely chopped	½ cabbage, coarsely chopped
1 lb (455g) potatoes, mashed	1 pound potatoes, mashed
3 oz (85g) Cheddar cheese, grated	¾ cupful Cheddar cheese, grated
Parsley (optional)	Parsley (optional)

1. Melt a little butter in a frying pan (skillet) and fry the onion until lightly browned.

2. Boil the cabbage until barely tender.

3. Mix the onion, potato and cabbage in a bowl and form the mixture into round cakes about 3 in. (7cm) in diameter and ½ in. (1cm) deep.

4. Melt the remaining butter in the frying pan (skillet) and fry the cakes until partly brown on each side (they will not brown evenly)..

5. Put a little cheese on each and place under a grill so that the cheese melts.

6. Serve hot, possibly garnished with parsley.

Eggless Tofu Scrambled Eggs

Imperial/Metric	American
2 onions, chopped	2 onions, chopped
2 tablespoonsful vegetable oil	2 tablespoonsful vegetable oil
1 lb (455g) tofu, mashed with a fork	2 cupsful tofu, mashed with a fork
1 tablespoonful soya sauce *or* to taste	1 tablespoonful soy sauce *or* to taste
½ teaspoonful turmeric	½ teaspoonful turmeric

1. Sauté the onions in the oil until they are transparent.

2. Add the mashed tofu, soya sauce and turmeric and continue to cook until the tofu is nicely browned.

Onions Almondine

Serves 1

Imperial/Metric	*American*
1 large onion, sliced	1 large onion, sliced
1 oz (30g) polyunsaturated margarine *or* butter	2½ tablespoonsful polyunsaturated margarine *or* butter
1 teaspoonful vegetable oil	1 teaspoonful vegetable oil
1 tablespoonful honey	1 tablespoonful honey
1 oz (30g) flaked almonds	¼ cupful slivered almonds
Seasoning to taste	Seasoning to taste

1. Fry the onion gently in the combined margarine and oil.

2. When the onion begins to colour, add the honey, nuts and seasoning, and cook it gently for 5 minutes more, or until the onion is ready to eat. (Watch to make sure it doesn't burn.)

Note: The onions may be served on wholemeal toast for a quick snack. If you have a spoonful of leftover cooked peas handy, add them to the mixture for extra protein and colour.

Pasta with Broccoli

Imperial/Metric	*American*
1 lb (455g) fresh broccoli, *or* frozen equivalent	1 pound fresh broccoli, *or* frozen equivalent
¾ lb (340g) wholemeal macaroni	3 cupsful wholewheat macaroni
3 tablespoonsful olive oil	3 tablespoonsful olive oil
1-2 cloves garlic, crushed	1-2 cloves garlic, crushed
Seasoning to taste	Seasoning to taste
1 oz (30g) roasted, flaked almonds	¼ cupful roasted, slivered almonds
Grated Parmesan cheese to serve (optional)	Grated Parmesan cheese to serve (optional)

1. Trim the broccoli, cut into large florets, and put into a pan of boiling salted water.

2. Cook for 5 minutes, then add the macaroni to the water and continue cooking for 10 minutes, or until the broccoli and macaroni are both just tender. Drain and keep warm.

3. In a frying pan (skillet) heat the oil and sauté the crushed garlic until it begins to colour.

4. Stir in the broccoli and macaroni and heat through stirring frequently. If the mixture seems very dry, add a drop of the water in which the broccoli was cooked.

5. Season to taste and transfer to a serving dish, or individual plates. Sprinkle with the nuts. Hand cheese around at the table, if liked.

Bananas and Rice

Imperial/Metric	American
2 onions, chopped	2 onions, chopped
Vegetable oil	Vegetable oil
1 lb 2 oz (500g) cooked, long-grain brown rice	3¾ cupsful cooked, long-grain brown rice
Soya sauce	Soy sauce
4 eggs	4 eggs
4 bananas	4 bananas
Parsley *or* carrot to garnish	Parsley *or* carrot to garnish

1. Sauté the onions in oil until soft.

2. Add the cooked brown rice and heat together, seasoning with soya sauce.

3. Fry the eggs in oil in another pan 'sunnyside up'.

4. Place the onion and rice mixture on individual plates, and form a pit in the middle. Fill the pit with one fried egg.

5. Slice the bananas lengthwise and fry in the oil in which the eggs have been fried. When they are slightly browned at the edges, remove and place the strips of banana on the rice around the pit containing the egg.

6. Garnish with parsley or strips of raw carrot and serve.

'Lincoln Stew'

Imperial/Metric	American
5 oz (140g) ham-flavoured soya chunks	1¼ cupsful ham-flavoured soy chunks
1 teaspoonful vegetable oil	1 teaspoonful vegetable oil
¾ pint (425ml) pea soup (leftover from previous meal *or* from soup mix)	2 cupsful pea soup (leftover from previous meal *or* from soup mix)
½ lb (225g) carrots	8 ounces carrots
Seasoning to taste	Seasoning to taste

1. Hydrate the soya chunks in boiling water to which the oil has been added.

2. In a saucepan, combine the soup, drained soya chunks, and chopped carrots. Season. Bring to the boil, stir well, then cover and simmer for 15 minutes.

3. Serve with mashed potatoes.

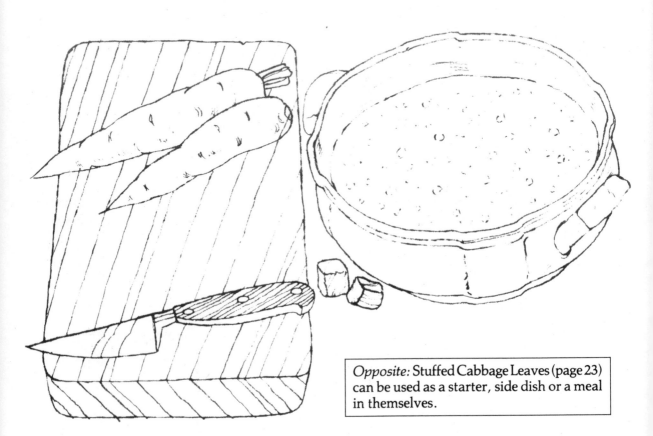

Opposite: Stuffed Cabbage Leaves (page 23) can be used as a starter, side dish or a meal in themselves.

Spanish Lentils

Imperial/Metric	American
½ lb (225g) lentils	1 cupful lentils
1 medium tin tomatoes	1 medium can tomatoes
1 onion, chopped	1 onion, chopped
2 sticks celery, chopped	2 stalks celery, chopped
1 green pepper, chopped	1 green pepper, chopped
3 teaspoonsful soya flour	3 teaspoonsful soy flour
2 tablespoonsful oil	2 tablespoonsful oil
Bay leaf	Bay leaf
Nutmeg	Nutmeg
Sea salt	Sea salt

1. Wash the lentils thoroughly and put them in a saucepan with all the other ingredients.

2. Cover and cook gently until the lentils are soft and fluffy (it may be necessary to add a little extra liquid during cooking).

3. Serve hot with vegetables or rice, or cold with salad.

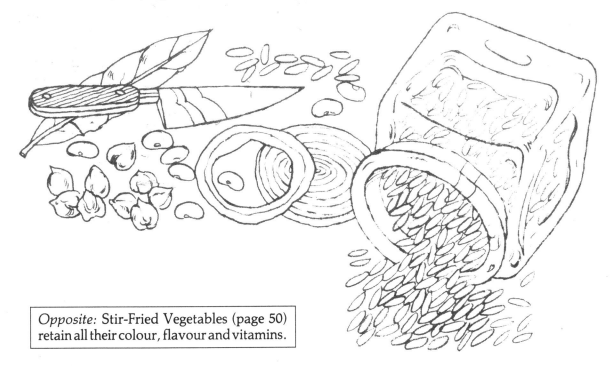

Opposite: Stir-Fried Vegetables (page 50) retain all their colour, flavour and vitamins.

Stir-Fried Vegetables

Serves 6

Imperial/Metric	American
2 medium carrots	2 medium carrots
2 peppers (red and green, if available)	2 peppers (red and green, if available)
12 dried mushrooms, soaked for at least 30 minutes	12 dried mushrooms, soaked for at least 30 minutes
4 sticks celery	4 stalks celery
Vegetable oil	Vegetable oil
2 cloves garlic, crushed	2 cloves garlic, crushed
1 medium onion, finely chopped	1 medium onion, finely chopped
4 slices ginger, finely chopped	4 slices ginger, finely chopped
1 tin bamboo shoot strip, drained	1 can bamboo shoot strip, drained
1 lb (455g) beansprouts, washed	1 pound beansprouts, washed
2 tablespoonsful sherry	2 tablespoonsful sherry
3 tablespoonsful soya sauce	3 tablespoonsful soy sauce
2 tablespoonsful sesame oil	2 tablespoonsful sesame oil

1.   Cut the carrots, peppers and mushrooms into matchstick size pieces.

2.   Slice the celery diagonally into 1 in. (2cm) segments.

3.   Heat the oil in a wok. Stir-fry the garlic, onion and ginger for 2 minutes.

4.   Add the mushrooms, carrots, drained bamboo shoots, celery and peppers. Finally add the beansprouts.

5.   After a minute or so, add the sherry and soya sauce. Cook over a high flame for 2 or 3 minutes.

6.   Just before serving add the sesame oil.

Illustrated opposite page 49.

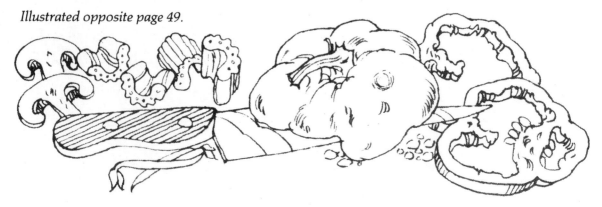

Spaghetti with Ricotta Sauce

Imperial/Metric	American
10 oz (285g) wholemeal spaghetti	10 ounces wholewheat spaghetti
6 oz (170g) Ricotta cheese	¾ cupful Ricotta cheese
2 oz (55g) grated Parmesan cheese	½ cupful grated Parmesan cheese
Good pinch of nutmeg	Good pinch of nutmeg
Seasoning to taste	Seasoning to taste
Fresh chives to garnish	Fresh chives to garnish

1. Plunge the spaghetti into boiling water and cook for 10 minutes, or until tender but still firm.

2. Meanwhile mash the Ricotta to make it creamy smooth, add the grated cheese, nutmeg, and seasoning to taste.

3. Drain the cooked spaghetti, put it into a bowl, and stir in the cheese mixture. Continue stirring until it has melted completely, then serve topped with a generous sprinkling of chopped chives.

Hot Rice-Stuffed Tomatoes

Imperial/Metric	American
2 large tomatoes	2 large tomatoes
½ oz (15g) polyunsaturated margarine	1 tablespoonful polyunsaturated margarine
1-2 oz (30-55g) mushrooms, finely chopped	½-¾ cupful finely chopped mushrooms
2 oz (55g) cooked brown rice	⅓ cupful cooked brown rice
1 oz (30g) cheese, grated	⅓ cupful grated cheese
Seasoning to taste	Seasoning to taste
1 tablespoonful tomato purée	1 tablespoonful tomato paste
Chives, chopped	Chives, chopped

1.   Wash and dry the tomatoes. Cut a slice from the round end, scoop out the seeds and pulp and chop them coarsely.

2.   Melt the margarine and sauté the mushrooms, then stir in the drained rice, tomato pulp, grated cheese and seasoning.

3.   Add enough tomato purée to moisten and mix it in well.

4.   Divide the mixture between each of the prepared tomato cases and arrange them in a shallow ovenproof dish, then cover each one with its own lid.

5.   Bake at 375°F/190°C (Gas Mark 5) for about 20 minutes, or until the tomatoes are puffed up and hot right through. Serve at once sprinkled with chives.

Note: Any leftover grain can be used instead of the rice, as may oats or even wholemeal breadcrumbs.

Entertaining from Around the World

Stroganoff

Serves 6

Imperial/Metric	American
½ lb (225g) tvp, rehydrated in white wine	2 cupsful tvp, rehydrated in white wine
4 medium onions, finely chopped	4 medium onions, finely chopped
3 cloves garlic, crushed	3 cloves garlic, crushed
3 oz (85g) butter	⅓ cupful butter
½ lb (225g) mushrooms, sliced	3 cupsful mushrooms, sliced
½ pint (285ml) soured cream	⅔ cupful soured cream
Sea salt and freshly ground pepper	Sea salt and freshly ground pepper
1 teaspoonful mild French mustard	1 teaspoonful mild French mustard

1. Strain off the excess liquid from the tvp, and reserve it.

2. Fry the onions and garlic in the butter for a few minutes.

3. Add the tvp and mushrooms. Stir and continue to cook over a medium heat for 5 minutes or so.

4. Add the soured cream, salt, pepper and mustard.

5. Simmer gently until the tvp is tender. Add the reserved liquid if necessary.

Illustrated opposite page 64.

Chow Mein

Serves 6

Imperial/Metric	American
1 lb (455g) noodles	3 cupsful noodles
Vegetable oil for frying	Vegetable oil for frying
1 medium onion, finely chopped	1 medium onion, finely chopped
2 cloves garlic, crushed	2 cloves garlic, crushed
½ lb (225g) white cabbage, shredded	8 ounces white cabbage, shredded
1 tin bamboo shoot strips, drained	1 can bamboo shoot strips, drained
4 tablespoonsful soya sauce	⅓ cupful soy sauce
20 dried mushrooms, soaked for at least 30 minutes	20 dried mushrooms, soaked for at least 30 minutes
2 tablespoonsful hoisin sauce	2 tablespoonsful hoisin sauce
4 tablespoonsful sherry	⅓ cupful sherry
Ratatouille sauce (see opposite)	Ratatouille sauce (see opposite)

1.   Place the noodles in boiling water to cover and soak for 10 minutes.

2.   Heat about 3 tablespoonsful of oil in a wok over a medium heat.

3.   Add the onion and garlic and stir-fry until transparent.

4.   Add the cabbage and bamboo shoots, stirring constantly for a further 3 minutes.

5.   Add the drained noodles and 2 tablespoonsful of soya sauce, and mix well. Stir on a medium heat for 3 or 4 minutes. The cabbage should still be crunchy.

6.   Spread the noodles on a hot serving dish and keep hot in the oven.

7.   Heat a little oil in the wok over a medium heat.

8.   Slice the mushrooms and fry them for 1 minute.

9.   Add 2 tablespoonsful of soya sauce, the hoisin sauce and sherry. Cook for 2 minutes.

10.   Pour the mushrooms over the centre of the noodles and the ratatouille sauce around the mushrooms.

11.   Return the dish to the oven and keep warm.

Ratatouille Sauce

Imperial/Metric	American
Vegetable oil for frying	Vegetable oil for frying
2 tablespoonsful salted black beans, dried *or* tinned	2 tablespoonsful salted black beans, dried *or* canned
2 medium onions, finely chopped	2 medium onions, finely chopped
2 cloves garlic, crushed	2 cloves garlic, crushed
2 slices root ginger, finely chopped	2 slices root ginger, finely chopped
1 red pepper, chopped	1 red pepper, chopped
14 oz (395g) tin tomatoes	1 medium can tomatoes
1 medium aubergine, cubed	1 medium eggplant, cubed
2 courgettes, sliced	2 zucchini, sliced
1 tablespoonful hoisin sauce	1 tablespoonful hoisin sauce
Vegetable stock	Vegetable stock
4 tablespoonsful soya sauce	⅓ cupful soy sauce
3 tablespoonsful sesame oil (optional)	3 tablespoonsful sesame oil (optional)

1. Heat the oil in a wok and add the beans, onion, garlic, ginger and red pepper.

2. Stir-fry for 5 minutes over a medium heat. Do not allow this to burn.

3. Add the tomatoes, aubergine (eggplant) cubes, courgettes (zucchini) and hoisin sauce. Fry for a further 5 minutes.

4. Add about 4 fl oz/120ml (½ cupful) of vegetable stock and simmer for about 20 minutes.

5. Add more stock if necessary (or use some red wine) along with the soya sauce.

6. Stir and simmer for a further 20 minutes or until the liquid begins to thicken.

7. Add the sesame oil, if used, before spooning the sauce over the chow mein.

55

Moroccan Rice Alicantina

Imperial/Metric	American
3-4 crushed cloves garlic	3-4 crushed cloves garlic
4 tablespoonsful vegetable oil	4 tablespoonsful vegetable oil
3 large green peppers, sliced	3 large green peppers, sliced
½ lb (225g) artichoke hearts	1¼ cupsful artichoke hearts
3 large tomatoes, chopped	3 large tomatoes, chopped
½ lb (225g) green beans, chopped	1¼ cupsful green beans, chopped
¾ lb (340g) long-grain brown rice	1⅔ cupsful long-grain brown rice
½ teaspoonful sea salt	½ teaspoonful sea salt
Pinch of freshly ground black pepper	Pinch of freshly ground black pepper
Pinch of turmeric	Pinch of turmeric
3 pints (1½ litres) vegetable stock *or* water	7½ cupsful vegetable stock *or* water

1. Fry the garlic in hot oil with the green peppers. Set aside.

2. Sauté artichokes, chopped tomatoes and beans.

3. Add rice, seasonings and turmeric.

4. Stir in the stock and cook briskly for 10 minutes, stirring constantly.

5. Simmer gently for approximately another 30 minutes until rice is cooked, then set to one side of the stove and allow to dry out.

6. Stir in the garlic and green pepper mixture and serve warm.

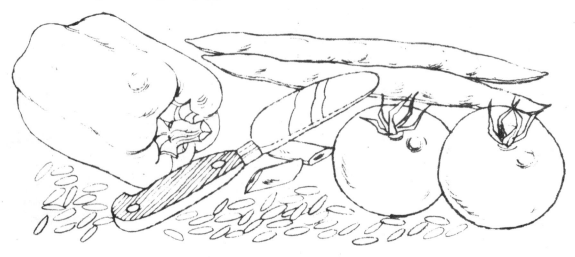

Quiche au Poivre

Imperial/Metric	*American*
Pastry to line an 8 in. (20cm) flan dish (see page 61)	Pastry to line an 8 inch flan dish (see page 61)
½ oz (15g) black peppercorns	½ ounce black peppercorns
1 oz (30g) polyunsaturated margarine	2½ tablespoonsful polyunsaturated margarine
½ pint (285ml) creamy milk	1⅓ cupsful creamy milk
3 egg yolks	3 egg yolks
Seasoning to taste	Seasoning to taste
4 oz (115g) cream *or* curd cheese	½ cupful cream *or* curd cheese

1.   Line the flan dish with the prepared and rolled out pastry, and bake blind at 400°F/200°C (Gas Mark 6) for 10 minutes.

2.   Meanwhile, crush the peppercorns coarsely and sauté them gently for just a few minutes in the melted margarine.

3.   Remove the pan from the heat and leave to cool for a few minutes, then add the creamy milk into which you have whisked the egg yolks; blend well; season to taste.

4.   Stir in the cream cheese until it dissolves. Pour the thick sauce into the partially cooked flan case.

5.   Bake the flan at 400°F/200°C (Gas Mark 6) for 20-30 minutes, or until set.

Illustrated opposite page 97.

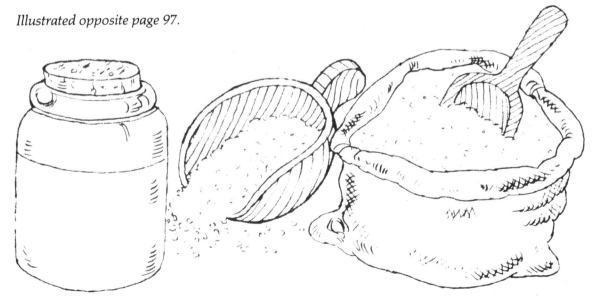

Home-Style Pizza

Dough:

Imperial/Metric	American
¼ oz (7g) dried yeast	½ teaspoonful dried yeast
Lukewarm water	Lukewarm water
½ lb (225g) plain wholemeal flour	2 cupsful plain wholewheat flour
Pinch of sea salt	Pinch of sea salt
1½ tablespoonsful vegetable oil	1½ tablespoonsful vegetable oil

Topping:

Imperial/Metric	American
1 lb (455g) tomatoes	1 pound tomatoes
6 oz (170g) Mozzarella cheese	6 ounces Mozzarella cheese
2 tablespoonsful vegetable oil	2 tablespoonsful vegetable oil
2 oz (55g) grated Parmesan cheese	½ cupful grated Parmesan cheese
Seasoning to taste	Seasoning to taste
2 teaspoonsful oregano	2 teaspoonsful oregano
4 oz (115g) mushrooms	2 cupsful mushrooms
12 black olives	12 black olives

1.   Dissolve the yeast in a drop of warm water, and set aside until the mixture begins to bubble.

2.   Sift together the flour and salt.

3.   Stir the oil into the yeast mixture, then add this to the flour with enough warm water to make a firm but pliable dough. Knead this on a floured board for a few minutes.

4.   Place in a bowl, cover with a damp cloth, and leave in a warm, draught-free spot for 30 minutes to 1 hour, or until well risen.

5.   Knead the dough again briefly, then divide into two pieces, shape them into balls, and flatten with a rolling pin to make two large circles.

6.   Place these on lightly greased baking sheets and cover with the chopped tomatoes.

7.   Slice the Mozzarella and divide the pieces between the two pizzas, arranging them on top of the tomatoes.

8.   Sprinkle a little of the oil over each of them, then Parmesan cheese, seasoning and oregano.

9.   Slice the mushrooms (unless you are using button mushrooms which look especially attractive as a topping), and arrange them on top of the pizzas together with the olives. Sprinkle the remaining oil over the mushrooms to prevent them getting too dry.

10.   Bake at 400°F/200°C (Gas Mark 6) for 25-30 minutes, or until the crust is crisp. Serve at once cut into wedges, or as two hearty individual pizzas.

Mushroom and Pepper Goulash

Imperial/Metric	American
2 oz (55g) polyunsaturated margarine *or* butter	¼ cupful polyunsaturated margarine *or* butter
1 onion	1 onion
2 red peppers	2 red peppers
¾ lb (340g) mushrooms	5 cupsful mushrooms
3 teaspoonsful paprika *or* to taste	3 teaspoonsful paprika *or* to taste
Seasoning to taste	Seasoning to taste
4 tablespoonsful vegetable stock *or* water	⅓ cupful vegetable stock *or* water
½ pint (285ml) plain yogurt *or* soured cream	1⅓ cupsful plain yogurt *or* soured cream
½ oz (15g) wholemeal flour	2 tablespoonsful wholewheat flour
2 or 3 hard-boiled eggs (optional)	2 or 3 hard-boiled eggs (optional)
Parsley to garnish	Parsley to garnish

1.   Melt the fat in a frying pan (skillet), add the sliced onion and peppers, and sauté for 5 minutes, or until the vegetables begin to soften.

2.   Stir in the sliced mushrooms and cook for 5 minutes more.

3.   Sprinkle in the paprika and seasoning, add the stock and stir well. Cover the pan and simmer the mixture for 10-15 minutes, or until the mushrooms are cooked.

4.   Mix together the yogurt and flour and stir them into the other ingredients, then heat gently until warmed through.

5.   Serve sprinkled with chopped hard-boiled eggs, if liked, and plenty of parsley.

Illustrated opposite page 64.

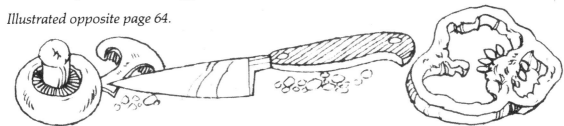

Lentils and Spinach

Serves 6

Imperial/Metric	American
½ lb (225g) brown lentils	1 cupful brown lentils
1 lb (455g) spinach	1 pound spinach
1 medium onion, finely chopped	1 medium onion, finely chopped
2 cloves garlic, crushed	2 cloves garlic, crushed
2 tablespoonsful vegetable oil	2 tablespoonsful vegetable oil
1 teaspoonful cumin seeds, ground	1 teaspoonful cumin seeds, ground
1 teaspoonful coriander seeds, ground	1 teaspoonful coriander seeds, ground
Sea salt and freshly ground black pepper	Sea salt and freshly ground black pepper
2 tablespoonsful lemon juice	2 tablespoonsful lemon juice

1. Wash the lentils and cook in water until tender. This will take about an hour.

2. If you are using fresh spinach, wash it and chop it finely. Put it into a saucepan with no water and cook gently and covered, for about 10 minutes. If you are using frozen spinach, thaw it and drain off excess liquid before using.

3. Fry the onions and garlic in the oil until they become transparent.

4. Add the cumin and coriander and cook for a further 3 minutes.

5. Stir in the lentils and spinach and, if necessary, cook until the dish is of a fairly thick consistency.

6. Season with the salt, pepper and lemon juice.

Illustrated opposite page 177.

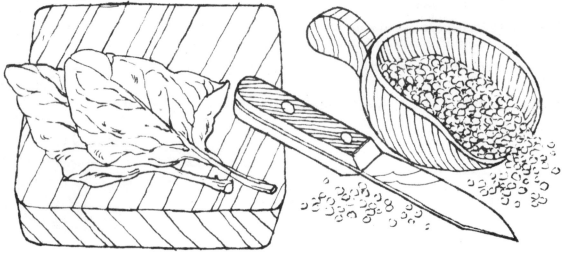

Tarte a l'Oignon Alsacienne

Serves 6
For pastry:

Imperial/Metric	American
¾ lb (340g) wholemeal flour	3 cupsful wholewheat flour
6 oz (170g) polyunsaturated margarine	⅔ cupful polyunsaturated margarine
Sea salt	Sea salt
Water to bind	Water to bind

For filling:

Imperial/Metric	American
6 medium onions, thinly sliced	6 medium onions, thinly sliced
2 oz (55g) butter	¼ cupful butter
4 eggs	4 eggs
½ pint (285ml) single cream	1⅓ cupsful light cream
Seasoning	Seasoning
A few caraway seeds	A few caraway seeds

1.   Make the shortcrust pastry by mixing well the flour and vegetable margarine with a pinch of sea salt. Add sufficient water to make a firm dough and set aside in a cool place while you make the filling.

2.   Fry the onions gently in the butter until they become transparent.

3.   Roll out the pastry and line a large flan tin. Cover the pastry with greaseproof paper and weigh down with a few dried beans.

4.   Bake the pastry case 'blind' in a hot oven at 400°F/200°C (Gas Mark 6) for 12 minutes.

5.   Spread the onions over the flan case.

6.   Combine the other ingredients in a blender.

7.   Pour this mixture over the onions.

8.   Bake at 350°F/180°C (Gas Mark 4) for 30 minutes or until browned on top.

Note: There are several variations on this recipe such as using cream cheese on top of the pie shell, so making layers of pastry, cream cheese, onion and cream topping.

Spinach and Ricotta Gnocchi

Imperial/Metric	American
½ lb (225g) cooked spinach, fresh *or* frozen	1 cupful cooked spinach, fresh *or* frozen
½ lb (225g) Ricotta cheese	1 cupful Ricotta cheese
4 oz (115g) grated Parmesan cheese	1 cupful grated Parmesan cheese
Pinch of nutmeg	Pinch of nutmeg
Seasoning to taste	Seasoning to taste
2 eggs	2 eggs
4 oz (115g) plain wholemeal flour	1 cupful plain wholewheat flour
2 oz (55g) polyunsaturated margarine	¼ cupful polyunsaturated margarine

1. Drain then chop the spinach.

2. Put into a bowl and mix well with the Ricotta cheese, half the Parmesan, nutmeg and seasoning.

3. When well blended, add the two beaten eggs.

4. Mix most of the flour into the mixture, then set aside to cool for 15-30 minutes.

5. Shape the dough into small balls; smooth the surface, and roll in the remaining flour.

6. Drop the gnocchi gently, a few at a time, in boiling salted water; simmer for 3-4 minutes, or until they rise to the surface.

7. Remove with a perforated spoon; drain on paper towels; keep hot whilst continuing to cook the rest of the gnocchi in the same way.

8. Arrange in a warmed serving dish; dot with margarine and sprinkle with the rest of the Parmesan cheese.

Illustrated opposite page 96.

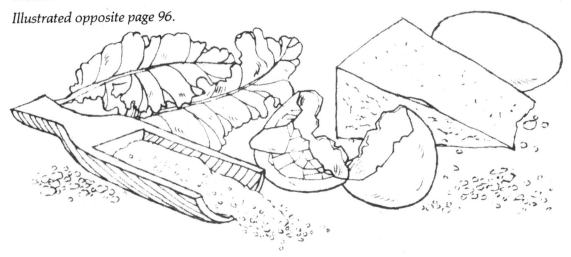

Moussaka

Serves 6

Imperial/Metric	American
2 lb (900g) aubergines	2 pounds eggplants
6 tablespoonsful olive oil (or more)	½ cupful olive oil (or more)
1 oz (30g) butter	2½ tablespoonsful butter
1 medium onion, finely chopped	1 medium onion, finely chopped
4 cloves garlic, crushed	4 cloves garlic, crushed
6 oz (170g) tvp, rehydrated in red wine	1½ cupsful tvp, rehydrated in red wine
14 oz (395g) tin tomatoes	1 medium can tomatoes
1 tablespoonful oregano	1 tablespoonful oregano
2 tablespoonsful parsley, finely chopped	2 tablespoonsful parsley, finely chopped
1 teaspoonful ground nutmeg	1 teaspoonful ground nutmeg
Sea salt and black pepper	Sea salt and black pepper
¼ pint (140ml) vegetable stock	⅔ cupful vegetable stock
4 oz (115g) tomato purée	⅔ cupful tomato paste
2 eggs	2 eggs
¼ pint (140ml) single cream	⅔ cupful light cream
6 tablespoonsful Parmesan, finely grated	6 tablespoonsful Parmesan, finely grated

1. Slice the aubergines (eggplants) fairly thinly, put them in a colander, sprinkle with sea salt and allow to stand for 30 minutes. Rinse and dry the slices.

2. Fry the aubergine (eggplant) slices in olive oil until browned on both sides. Drain on absorbent paper and put aside.

3. Melt the butter and fry the onion and garlic until transparent.

4. Add the tvp and the tomatoes along with the oregano, parsley and nutmeg. Season well with sea salt and black pepper.

5. Simmer for 20-30 minutes, adding more liquid if necessary.

6. Grease a casserole dish and arrange in it alternate layers of aubergine (eggplant) and tvp, starting and finishing with aubergine (eggplant). Sprinkle each layer with a tablespoonful of Parmesan.

7. Combine the tomato purée (paste) and stock and pour this into the casserole.

8. Bake in a moderate oven at 350°F/180°C (Gas Mark 4) for about 30 minutes.

9. Meanwhile blend the eggs and cream and season with sea salt and pepper.

10. Pour this mixture over the dish and sprinkle with the remaining Parmesan and bake for a further 15-20 minutes until the sauce is set and golden brown.

Turkish Pilaff

Serves 6

Imperial/Metric	American
2 medium onions, finely chopped	2 medium onions, finely chopped
3 cloves garlic, crushed	3 cloves garlic, crushed
1 lb (455g) long-grain brown rice	2 cupsful long-grain brown rice
4 tablespoonsful vegetable oil	⅓ cupful vegetable oil
3 bay leaves	3 bay leaves
14 oz (395g) tin tomatoes	1 medium can tomatoes
2 tablespoonsful tomato purée	2 tablespoonsful tomato paste
4 oz (115g) dried apricots	¾ cupful dried apricots
2 oz (55g) sultanas	⅓ cupful golden seedless raisins
2 oz (55g) almonds, blanched and shredded	½ cupful almonds, blanched and shredded
Sea salt and freshly ground black pepper	Sea salt and freshly ground black pepper
1 pint (570ml) vegetable stock	2½ cupsful vegetable stock
Coriander leaves	Cilantro leaves

1. Fry the onions and garlic in the oil until they become transparent.

2. Add the rice and continue to fry for 3 minutes, stirring constantly.

3. Add the remaining ingredients except the coriander (cilantro) leaves, bring to the boil, then simmer, covered, for 45 minutes.

4. Serve garnished with the coriander (cilantro) leaves.

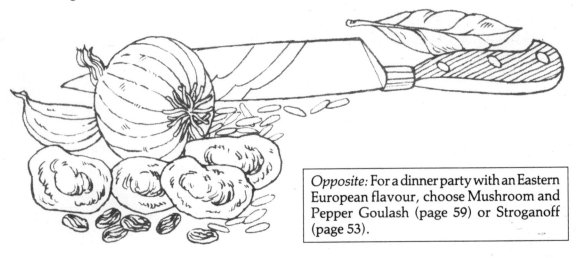

Opposite: For a dinner party with an Eastern European flavour, choose Mushroom and Pepper Goulash (page 59) or Stroganoff (page 53).

Deep-Fried Rice Balls

Imperial/Metric	American
6 oz (170g) brown rice	¾ cupful brown rice
1 pint (570ml) vegetable stock *or* water	2½ cupsful vegetable stock *or* water
2 tomatoes	2 tomatoes
Seasoning to taste	Seasoning to taste
2 eggs	2 eggs
4 oz (115g) Mozzarella cheese	4 ounces Mozzarella cheese
3-4 oz (85-115g) fine wholemeal breadcrumbs	1½-2 cupsful fine wholewheat breadcrumbs
Oil for frying	Oil for frying

1. Add the rice to the boiling stock or water, stir in the peeled and finely chopped tomatoes and then simmer the mixture until the rice is cooked. Add seasoning. Drain well and leave to cool.

2. Beat the eggs and add them to the rice mixture. Put a tablespoonful of it onto the palm of your hand, put a cube or piece of cheese on top, then mould the rice around the cheese to form a small ball. Roll this very carefully in the breadcrumbs to make a light, even coating. Use up the rest of the ingredients in the same way.

3. Deep fry the balls a few at a time in a deep pan of hot oil, turning them frequently, until the outsides are golden and crisp — the cheese inside will melt to a thick cream. Drain the rice balls on paper towels and serve whilst still hot.

Note: Make these when you have plain rice or risotto left over from a previous meal, and cut the preparation time in half. Just make sure there are no large pieces of vegetables in the rice which may tend to make the mixture more crumbly.

Opposite: Swiss Cheese Fondue (page 68) is perfect for an informal dinner party.

65

Aubergines in Coconut Cream

Serves 6

Imperial/Metric	American
2 large aubergines	2 large eggplants
1 medium onion, thinly sliced	1 medium onion, thinly sliced
1 hot red pepper, finely chopped	1 hot red pepper, finely chopped
2 oz (55g) Parmesan cheese	½ cupful Parmesan cheese
Seasoning	Seasoning
7 oz (200g) block coconut cream	7 ounce block coconut cream

1.   Slice the aubergines (eggplants) thinly. You can salt them and allow some of the bitter juices to flow out before you rinse and use them.

2.   Arrange layers of aubergines (eggplants), onions, peppers, Parmesan and seasoning in a greased ovenproof dish.

3.   Meanwhile, melt the coconut cream in about 2 pints (1 litre) of water and stir until it is smooth.

4.   Pour the coconut cream over the aubergines.

5.   Bake at 350°F/180°C (Gas Mark 4) for about an hour, covered, or until the aubergines (eggplants) are tender.

Stuffed Cho-Chos

If served as a starter, or as a principal dish in the main course, allow one cho-cho per person. If served as a side dish, allow half a cho-cho per person.

Imperial/Metric	*American*
6 cho-chos*	6 cho-chos*
4 tablespoonsful vegetable oil	⅓ cupful vegetable oil
4 medium onions, finely chopped	4 medium onions, finely chopped
2 cloves garlic, crushed	2 cloves garlic, crushed
4 oz (115g) tvp, rehydrated in red wine *or* stock	1 cupful tvp, rehydrated in red wine *or* stock
14 oz (395g) tin tomatoes	1 medium can tomatoes
1 tablespoonful chilli sauce or whole grain mustard	1 tablespoonful chilli sauce or whole grain mustard
3 tablespoonsful soya sauce	3 tablespoonsful soy sauce
Black pepper	Black pepper
4 tablespoonsful Parmesan cheese, finely grated	4 tablespoonsful Parmesan cheese, finely grated

1. Boil the cho-chos in salted water for 30 minutes until tender.

2. Cut the cho-chos in half lengthwise.

3. Scoop out the edible seed and then the pulp.

4. Mash the pulp.

5. Heat the oil and fry the onion and garlic until transparent.

6. Add the tvp and fry for a further 5 minutes.

7. Stir in the tomatoes and cho-cho pulp and add the seasonings including the chilli sauce or mustard, depending on availability and personal taste. Cook for 10 to 15 minutes until the tvp is tender.

8. Place the filling in the cho-cho shells and sprinkle with Parmesan cheese.

9. Bake at 350°F/180°C (Gas Mark 4) for 15 minutes until lightly browned.

* Cho-cho is a pear-shaped vegetable of the marrow (squash) family, often used in West Indian cookery.

Swiss Cheese Fondue

Imperial/Metric	*American*
1 clove garlic	1 clove garlic
Up to ¾ pint (425ml) white wine	2 cupsful white wine
14 oz (395g) Gruyère cheese, grated	3½ cupsful Gruyère cheese, grated
7 oz (200g) Emmenthal cheese, grated	1¾ cupsful Emmenthal cheese, grated
2 tablespoonsful kirsch	2 tablespoonsful kirsch
1 tablespoonful arrowroot	1 tablespoonful arrowroot
1 tablespoonful lemon juice	1 tablespoonful lemon juice
Nutmeg, grated	Nutmeg, grated
Pepper	Pepper

For dipping:

Imperial/Metric	*American*
Cubed wholemeal bread	Cubed wholewheat bread
1 lb (455g) button mushrooms (fried in butter until tender)	8 cupsful button mushrooms (fried in butter until tender)
Potato balls (see below)	Potato balls (see below)

1. Rub the fondue pot well with garlic.

2. Heat the wine in a saucepan and gradually sprinkle into it the cheese, stirring constantly.

3. Mix the kirsch with the arrowroot and lemon juice and pour into the cheese and wine mixture.

4. Season with pepper and a little grated nutmeg.

Illustrated opposite page 65.

Potato Balls

Imperial/Metric	*American*
1 lb (455g) mashed potato	2½ cupsful mashed potato
2 egg yolks	2 egg yolks
2 tablespoonsful wholemeal flour	2 tablespoonsful wholewheat flour
Sea salt	Sea salt
3 tablespoonsful fine wholemeal breadcrumbs	3 tablespoonsful fine wholewheat breadcrumbs
Vegetable oil for deep-frying	Vegetable oil for deep-frying

1.   Mix the mashed potato with most of the egg yolk and flour. Add a little salt.

2.   Shape into smallish balls about 1½ in. (3cm) across.

3.   Dip each ball in the remaining egg yolk and roll in breadcrumbs.

4.   Deep-fry in the oil until brown.

Illustrated between pages 96 and 97.

Rice with Truffles

Truffles are a kind of mushroom that grow underground in just a few parts of Europe. Because they are so rare, they are very expensive, and are therefore treated with great respect when used in a dish. This simple recipe is a popular way of serving the delicately flavoured white truffle.

Imperial/Metric	American
10 oz (285g) brown rice*	1¼ cupsful brown rice*
1½ pints (¾ litre) vegetable stock	3¾ cupsful vegetable stock
4-6 oz (115-170g) freshly grated Parmesan cheese	1-1½ cupsful freshly grated Parmesan cheese
2 oz (55g) unsalted butter	¼ cupful unsalted butter
Seasoning to taste	Seasoning to taste
White truffles**	White truffles**

1.   Simmer the rice in the vegetable stock until it is perfectly cooked — tender but not mushy.

2.   Drain, and stir in the cheese, butter and seasoning.

3.   When the cheese and butter have melted to make the rice creamy smooth, transfer it to a warmed serving dish, and top with paper-thin slices of the raw truffles. Serve at once.

* Although brown rice is more nutritious, it has a stronger flavour than the white variety, which may diminish the subtle garlic-like taste of the truffles.

** Use as many truffles as you can find and afford. Even one truffle added to rice in this way makes it a very special dish.

Summer Rice Dish

Imperial/Metric	American
2 tablespoonsful vegetable oil	2 tablespoonsful vegetable oil
1 onion	1 onion
1 medium courgette	1 medium zucchini
4 oz (115g) broad beans	⅔ cupful Windsor beans
4 oz (115g) green beans	4 ounces green beans
½ small cabbage	½ small cabbage
½ lb (225g) brown rice	1 cupful brown rice
1¼ pints (650ml) vegetable stock	3¼ cupsful vegetable stock
2 tomatoes, quartered	2 tomatoes, quartered
Seasoning to taste	Seasoning to taste
1 oz (30g) polyunsaturated margarine *or* butter	2½ tablespoonsful polyunsaturated margarine *or* butter
Chives to garnish	Chives to garnish
Grated cheese (optional)	Grated cheese (optional)

1. Heat the oil in a large pan and gently fry the sliced onion for a few minutes.

2. Add the sliced courgette (zucchini), the broad beans (Windsor beans), chopped green beans, and shredded cabbage, and mix well.

3. Cover the pan and cook gently for 5 minutes more.

4. Stir in the rice and cook briefly until it becomes translucent.

5. Pour in the stock, and continue cooking until the rice is tender and the liquid has been absorbed.

6. Add the quartered tomatoes and leave the pan over a gentle heat for just a minute more so that they are heated through but not cooked.

7. Off the heat, stir in the margarine so that it melts to give the rice a creamy coating. Tip it into a warmed dish, top with chopped chives, and serve immediately. Grated cheese could be handed round at the table.

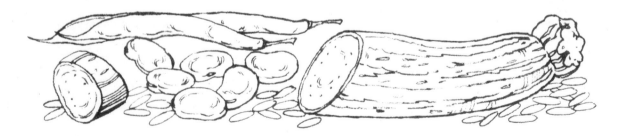

Tipperary Pie

Serves 6

Imperial/Metric	American
6 oz (170g) tvp, rehydrated in red wine *or* vegetable stock	1½ cupsful tvp, rehydrated in red wine *or* vegetable stock
1 leek, chopped	1 leek, chopped
2 carrots, diced	2 carrots, diced
½ swede, diced	½ rutabaga, diced
1 parsnip, diced	1 parsnip, diced
Sea salt	Sea salt
Freshly ground black pepper	Freshly ground black pepper
1 teaspoonful mixed herbs	1 teaspoonful mixed herbs
3 tablespoonsful soya sauce	3 tablespoonsful soy sauce

For the pastry:

Imperial/Metric	American
½ lb (225g) wholemeal flour	2 cupsful wholewheat flour
2 oz (55g) polyunsaturated margarine	¼ cupful polyunsaturated margarine
2 oz (55g) vegetable fat	5 tablespoonsful vegetable fat
1 teaspoonful sea salt	1 teaspoonful sea salt
1 teaspoonful baking powder	1 teaspoonful baking powder
Water	Water

1. Soak the tvp in wine or stock (or stout) for at least 1 hour.

2. Put it in a pan with the vegetables and seasoning.

3. Simmer for 30 minutes adding further liquid if necessary.

4. Make the pastry by mixing the flour with the fat, salt and baking powder. Add enough water to make the pastry of the right consistency.

5. Roll out the pastry to fit a casserole. Fill with the tvp mixture and put a pastry lid on.

6. Bake at 350°F/180°C (Gas Mark 4) for 50 minutes.

Tofu Tamale Pie

Imperial/Metric	American
2 onions, chopped	2 onions, chopped
2 green peppers, chopped	2 green peppers, chopped
3 cloves garlic, minced	3 cloves garlic, minced
3 tablespoonsful vegetable oil	3 tablespoonsful vegetable oil
1½ lb (680g) tofu	3 cupsful tofu
2 lb (900g) tomatoes, fresh *or* tinned	2 pounds tomatoes, fresh *or* canned
¾ lb (340g) sweetcorn	2 cupsful sweetcorn
⅓ pint (200ml) water	1 cupful water
2 tablespoonsful chilli powder	2 tablespoonsful chilli powder
2 tablespoonsful soya sauce *or* to taste	2 tablespoonsful soy sauce *or* to taste
1 teaspoonful cumin	1 teaspoonful cumin
5 oz (140g) maize flour	1 cupful cornmeal

1.   Sauté the onions, peppers and garlic in the oil, using a large ovenproof casserole.

2.   Add the remaining ingredients, place the casserole in the oven and bake it at 350°F/180°C (Gas Mark 4) for about 1 hour. (If desired, put sliced cheese on top, although this dish is good without as well.)

Brinjal and Tomato Curry

Imperial/Metric	American
1 red pepper, chopped	1 red pepper, chopped
1 tablespoonful ghee *or* vegetable fat	1 tablespoonful ghee *or* vegetable fat
1 brinjal (aubergine), diced	1 brinjal (eggplant), diced
1 onion, sliced	1 onion, sliced
3 tomatoes, chopped	3 tomatoes, chopped
1 teaspoonful turmeric	1 teaspoonful turmeric
½ teaspoonful cumin	½ teaspoonful cumin
¼ teaspoonful chilli	¼ teaspoonful chilli
½ teaspoonful asafoetida*	½ teaspoonful asafoetida*
Sea salt to taste	Sea salt to taste

1.   Fry the pepper in the fat until tender, then set it aside. Do the same with the brinjal.

2.   Fry the onion until golden brown, add the tomatoes and mix in the turmeric, pepper, cumin, chilli, asafoetida and salt.

3.   Stir well and cook the mixture for 5 minutes at a moderate heat. Add the brinjal, mix and cook gently for 5 minutes. Serve the curry with rice and pickles.

Note: One advantage of the brinjal over many vegetables is that it cooks through rapidly; such dishes can therefore be prepared quickly.

* A popular curry spice available from most Indian food shops.

Bagathed Khichiri

Imperial/Metric	*American*
2 large onions	2 large onions
1 tablespoonful ghee *or* vegetable fat	1 tablespoonful ghee *or* vegetable fat
¾ lb (340g) brown rice	1½ cupsful brown rice
4 oz (115g) red lentils	½ cupful red lentils
1 teaspoonful sea salt	1 teaspoonful sea salt
1 teaspoonful turmeric	1 teaspoonful turmeric
½ in. (1cm) piece of green ginger	½ inch piece of green ginger
1 teaspoonful *panch phora* *	1 teaspoonful *panch phora* *
1 tablespoonful onion stalks *or* chives	1 tablespoonful onion stalks *or* chives
Parsley and paprika to garnish	Parsley and paprika to garnish

1.   Slice the onions finely and fry half of them in the ghee, with the rice and lentils, for about 5 minutes.

2.   Add the salt, cover the mixture with boiling water, add the turmeric, ginger and *panch phora* and simmer very gently until the rice is cooked through and the water has evaporated.

3.   Spoon the mixture onto a warm flat dish, top with fried onions, parsley and paprika. Serve with lime or brinjal pickle.

* A flavouring sold in packets that contains combinations of whole seeds that impart a flavour different from anything you have tasted.

Illustrated opposite page 113.

Egg Pilau

Imperial/Metric	American
4 eggs	4 eggs
6 onions	6 onions
4 oz (115g) ghee *or* vegetable fat	½ cupful ghee *or* vegetable fat
10 peppercorns	10 peppercorns
5 or 6 green beans	5 or 6 green beans
4 blades mace	4 blades mace
10 cloves	10 cloves
Seeds of 10 cardamoms	Seeds of 10 cardamoms
1 in. (2.5cm) piece of ginger	1 inch piece of ginger
10-12 curry leaves	10-12 curry leaves
6 oz (170g) brown rice	¾ cupful brown rice
6 cloves garlic	6 cloves garlic

1. Boil the eggs until hard; shell them, slice them into halves and set them aside.

2. Fry 4 of the sliced onions in the ghee with the peppercorns, green beans, mace, cloves, cardamoms, ginger and curry leaves for 2 minutes.

3. Place the rice in a saucepan with a close-fitting lid. Add the onions and spices and just cover them with water.

4. Bring the water to the boil and then simmer until the rice is cooked. (If more water is needed, add some from time to time.)

5. Remove the pan from the heat and set aside with the lid on.

6. Fry the remaining onions and garlic in a little vegetable fat until brown.

7. Place the rice, spices and vegetables on a large flat dish and garnish with the fried onions, garlic and a little chopped parsley. Serve with yogurt and sweet chutney.

Note: Remove the curry leaves before serving.

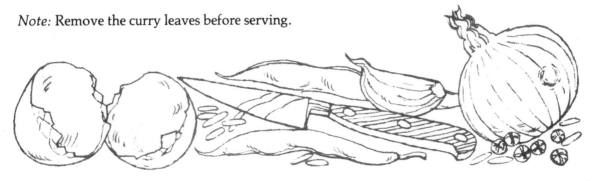

The following side dishes make a good accompaniment to any curry:

Chapattis

Imperial/Metric	American
1 lb (455g) wholemeal flour	4 cupsful wholewheat flour
A little sea salt	A little sea salt
Approx. ½ pint (285ml) water	1⅓ cupsful water
1 teaspoonful ghee	1 teaspoonful ghee

1.   Put 2 oz/55g (½ cupful) of flour to one side. Mix the remaining salt and flour thoroughly.

2.   Make a hollow in the centre of the flour and add the water gradually, working it in well until the water is absorbed and the dough elastic.

3.   Knead the dough well for about 5 minutes, then set aside and cover it with a damp piece of muslin for 30 minutes or more.

4.   Knead lightly once more, then break off pieces of dough and shape them into small balls.

5.   Dust each one with a little of the extra flour and roll it out very thinly.

6.   Heat a frying pan (skillet), add the ghee, place the chapatti in it and when the first bubbles rise in the flour, turn the chapatti, using a spatula or by hand. After about 30 seconds, press down the edges and gently rotate the disc.

7.   Lift the chapatti with a fish slice and hold it directly over the heat for a second or two. The chapatti should swell and is then ready to serve. These are tricky to make at first, but once you have got the knack they can be made easily and quickly.

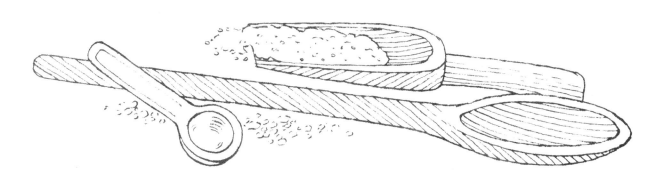

Green Mango Bhurta

Imperial/Metric	American
1 large green mango	1 large green mango
1 teaspoonful raw cane sugar	1 teaspoonful raw cane sugar
½ teaspoonful each ground ginger and sea salt	½ teaspoonful each ground ginger and sea salt
¼ teaspoonful ground red chilli	¼ teaspoonful ground red chilli
6 fresh mint leaves	6 fresh mint leaves
1 teaspoonful cider vinegar	1 teaspoonful cider vinegar

1.   Peel and remove the flesh from the mango, then mash it into a pulp using a pestle and mortar.

2.   Mix the sugar with the pulp, then add the salt, ginger, chilli, and mint leaves, using the vinegar to bind them. (If the mango tastes too acid, add a little more sugar.)

Note: A similar bhurta can also be made with a cooking apple instead of a mango. Of course, the flavour will be rather different. A little tomato juice may be added.

Cucumber Raita

Imperial/Metric	American
Sea salt to taste	Sea salt to taste
½ pint (285ml) natural yogurt	1⅓ cupsful natural yogurt
½ cucumber, finely chopped	½ cucumber, finely chopped
¼ teaspoonful freshly ground black pepper	¼ teaspoonful freshly ground black pepper
½ green chilli, chopped	½ green chilli, chopped
Seeds of 1 cardamom	Seeds of 1 cardamom
1 small onion, finely chopped	1 small onion, finely chopped
A few coriander leaves, chopped	A few cilantro leaves, chopped
Parsley to garnish	Parsley to garnish

1.   Add a little salt to the yogurt and mix thoroughly with the cucumber, black pepper, chilli, cardamom seeds and onion.

2.   Garnish with the coriander (cilantro) leaves and parsley.

Illustrated opposite page 113.

Food for Patios and Picnics

Millet and Vegetable Croquettes

Imperial/Metric	American
4 oz (115g) millet	½ cupful millet
½ pint (285ml) water	1⅓ cupful water
Approx. 6 oz (170g) mixed cooked vegetables	Approx. ¾ cupful mixed cooked vegetables
2 oz (55g) wholemeal flour	½ cupful wholewheat flour
Soya sauce	Soy sauce
Seasoning to taste	Seasoning to taste
Vegetable oil for frying	Vegetable oil for frying

1. Cook the millet in the water until it is thick and porridge-like in consistency. Set aside to cool.

2. Chop the vegetables up small and add them to the millet with the flour, soya sauce and seasoning, blending well.

3. Divide the mixture into croquettes, roll them in a little extra flour, and deep-fry them. Drain well before serving hot or cold.

Note: This recipe is an ideal way to use up leftovers. You can replace the millet with rice or other grains, add an egg or some cheese for a change.

Salad Roulade

Imperial/Metric	American
½ **Webbs lettuce**	½ **Webbs lettuce**
2 tomatoes	**2 tomatoes**
1 oz (30g) mushrooms	½ **cupful mushrooms**
2 small spring onions	**2 small scallions**
A little Parmesan cheese, grated	**A little Parmesan cheese, grated**
6 oz (170g) grated cheese	1½ **cupsful grated cheese**
2 oz (55g) fresh wholemeal breadcrumbs	**1 cupful fresh wholewheat breadcrumbs**
4 eggs	**4 eggs**
¼ **pint (140ml) single cream**	⅔ **cupful light cream**
Seasoning to taste	**Seasoning to taste**
1 teaspoonful ready-made mustard	**1 teaspoonful ready-made mustard**
2 tablespoonsful warm water	**2 tablespoonsful warm water**
4 tablespoonsful mayonnaise	**4 tablespoonsful mayonnaise**
Parsley to garnish	**Parsley to garnish**

1. Heat the oven to 400°F/200°C (Gas Mark 6).

2. Wash and dry the lettuce and shred it finely, then wash and slice the tomatoes and mushrooms thinly. Chop the spring onions (scallions).

3. Line a Swiss-roll tin (approx. 13 x 9 inches/33 x 23 cm) with greaseproof paper and sprinkle with the grated Parmesan.

4. Mix the grated cheese and breadcrumbs together in a bowl.

5. Separate the eggs and add the yolks to the cheese and breadcrumb mixture. Also add the cream, seasoning and mustard and stir in the warm water to make a fairly soft mixture.

6. Whisk the egg whites until they form peaks and fold them carefully into the mixture.

7. Spread the mixture carefully onto the Swiss-roll tin and bake it for 10-15 minutes until it rises and is firm to the touch.

8. Allow to cool slightly and then place a clean, damp tea-towel over the top until absolutely cold.

9. Sprinkle a sheet of greaseproof paper generously with grated Parmesan. Loosen the edges of the roulade and tip it gently onto the paper.

10. Spread the roulade with mayonnaise and then lay the lettuce, sliced mushrooms, onions and tomatoes on top. Season well and using the greaseproof paper, roll the roulade up as you would a Swiss-roll. Lay it on a plate and garnish with chopped parsley. Serve the roulade cut into slices.

Illustrated opposite page 80.

Potato and Broad Bean Salad

Imperial/Metric	American
½ lb (225g) small potatoes	8 ounces small potatoes
½ lb (225g) fresh *or* frozen broad beans	8 ounces fresh *or* frozen Windsor beans
½ small onion	½ small onion
1 tablespoonful lemon juice	1 tablespoonful lemon juice
3 tablespoonsful olive oil	3 tablespoonsful olive oil
Parsley	Parsley
1 tablespoonful capers	1 tablespoonful capers
Seasoning to taste	Seasoning to taste

1. Scrub the potatoes, then steam them in their skins until just cooked — they should still be firm. Peel them if you like, then cut into cubes and put them into a bowl.

2. At the same time, cook the beans in boiling, salted water for about 15 minutes, or until tender. Drain well, then mix with the potatoes.

3. Whilst the vegetables are still warm add the finely chopped onion, the lemon juice and oil, chopped parsley and capers, and seasoning to taste.

4. Chill well before serving garnished with extra parsley.

Illustrated opposite page 81.

Aubergine Salad

Serves 6

Imperial/Metric	American
2 large aubergines, cubed	2 large eggplants, cubed
Sea salt and pepper	Sea salt and pepper
Olive oil for frying	Olive oil for frying
6 sticks celery, chopped	6 stalks celery, chopped
14 oz (395g) tin tomatoes	1 medium can tomatoes
⅓ pint (200ml) red wine vinegar	¾ cupful red wine vinegar
2 tablespoonsful sultanas	2 tablespoonsful golden seedless raisins
4 oz (115g) green olives, stoned	4 ounces green olives, stoned
3 tablespoonsful capers	3 tablespoonsful capers
1 tablespoonful honey	1 tablespoonful honey
3 lemon wedges	3 lemon wedges

1. Cube the aubergines (eggplants) and sprinkle with sea salt. Leave in a bowl with a heavy plate on top for 1 hour or so.

2. Wash and drain the aubergines (eggplants) and fry the cubes, a few at a time, in the olive oil until they are tender.

3. Fry the celery then add the tomatoes and the remaining ingredients including the aubergines (eggplants).

4. Cook gently for 10 minutes. Serve hot or cold as required, garnished with lemon wedges.

Opposite: Lunch for a Summer outing. Salad Roulade (page 78) and Tabbouleh (page 95).

Mixed Bean Salad

Imperial/Metric	American
4 oz (115g) dried kidney beans	¾ cupful dried kidney beans
4 oz (115g) chick peas	½ cupful garbanzo beans
4 oz (115g) haricot beans	½ cupful navy beans
4 oz (115g) brown rice, cooked	¾ cupful brown rice, cooked
1 lb (455g) sliced green beans	1 pound sliced green beans
2 onions	2 onions

Vinaigrette:

Imperial/Metric	American
½ pint (285ml) olive oil	1¼ cupsful olive oil
4 fl oz (120ml) wine vinegar	½ cupful wine vinegar
1 clove garlic, crushed	1 clove garlic, crushed
Sea salt and freshly ground black pepper	Sea salt and freshly ground black pepper
Mustard	Mustard

1.   Soak pulses overnight, then cook for 1½-2 hours — separately if convenient.

2.   Cook green beans in salted water until tender but not too soft.

3.   Slice onions into rings.

4.   Drain the beans.

5.   Mix all the salad ingredients in a bowl.

6.   Combine the ingredients for the vinaigrette dressing in a screw-top jar and shake. Pour over salad ingredients whilst still warm, then set aside to cool.

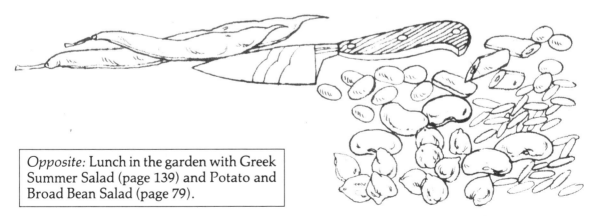

Opposite: Lunch in the garden with Greek Summer Salad (page 139) and Potato and Broad Bean Salad (page 79).

'Sausage' Rolls

For puff pastry:

Imperial/Metric	American
4 oz (115g) plain wholemeal flour	1 cupful plain wholewheat flour
Pinch of sea salt	Pinch of sea salt
Squeeze of lemon juice	Squeeze of lemon juice
Water to mix	Water to mix
4 oz (115g) polyunsaturated margarine *or* butter	½ cupful polyunsaturated margarine *or* butter

For filling:

Imperial/Metric	American
1 tin or packet of 'sausage' nut mix	1 can or pack of 'sausage' nut mix
1 egg, beaten, or water	1 egg, beaten, or water

1. Place the flour in a bowl and add the salt, lemon juice, and just enough water to make a soft dough.

2. On a floured board, roll the dough out to an oblong.

3. Cut the fat into small pieces and dot them over the centre third of the dough.

4. Fold one third over to cover the fat, then the other third and seal the edges. Turn the dough and roll it out to an oblong again.

5. Repeat this process of rolling and folding the dough seven times, wrapping it in cling film and putting it in the fridge for 10 minutes at least between each rolling. (The results will, in fact, be better if you work in a cool room with cool hands and utensils!)

6. Either cut or shape the 'sausages' into eight 2 in. (5cm) pieces.

7. Roll half the prepared pastry to a strip about 2 in. (5cm) wide and place the sausages along it, then cover them with another strip of pastry.

8. Dampen the edges either with egg or water and press them down firmly, then cut between the sausages and also seal these new edges.

9. Make one or two slits on the top of each roll, and brush — if liked — with more egg. Place the rolls on a baking tray and bake at 425°F/220°C (Gas Mark 7) for about 20 minutes or until the pastry is cooked. (These may be eaten hot or cold.)

Note: As puff pastry is a rather complicated process, it might be worth making extra and keeping it in the freezer to use on another occasion. You can, of course, use shortcrust pastry for different, but equally tasty, sausage rolls.

Celery Flan Amandine

For base:

Imperial/Metric	American
2 oz (55g) ground almonds	½ cupful ground almonds
4 oz (115g) plain wholemeal flour	1 cupful plain wholewheat flour
3 oz (85g) polyunsaturated margarine	⅓ cupful polyunsaturated margarine
Cold water to mix	Cold water to mix

For filling:

Imperial/Metric	American
1 large head of celery	1 large head of celery
1 small onion	1 small onion
2 oz (55g) polyunsaturated margarine	¼ cupful polyunsaturated margarine
1 oz (30g) plain wholemeal flour	¼ cupful plain wholewheat flour
½ pint (285ml) cream *or* creamy milk	1⅓ cupsful cream *or* creamy milk
3 oz (85g) roasted, flaked almonds	¾ cupful roasted, slivered almonds
Seasoning to taste	Seasoning to taste

1. Combine the flour and ground almonds, then rub in the margarine.

2. Add enough water to make a firm dough; knead briefly, then wrap in aluminium foil or clingfilm and chill in the fridge.

3. Roll out the chilled pastry, line a flan dish, and bake 'blind' for 20 minutes at 400°F/200°C (Gas Mark 6). Cool slightly.

4. Clean the celery and slice diagonally in small pieces; chop the onion as finely as possible; cook celery and onion in the melted margarine for 10-15 minutes, stirring occasionally.

5. When celery is just tender, sprinkle in the flour, add the cream and stir to make a thick sauce. Remove from heat.

6. Spoon the mixture into the flan case, smooth the top, and scatter generously with the nuts.

7. Bake at 350°F/180°C (Gas Mark 4) for about 10 minutes more. Serve hot.

Illustrated opposite page 160.

Sweet-Sour Vegetables

Imperial/Metric	American
2 large aubergines	2 large eggplants
Sea salt	Sea salt
6 tablespoonsful olive oil	½ cupful olive oil
1 large onion	1 large onion
4 large sticks celery, parboiled	4 large stalks celery, parboiled
1 lb (455g) tomatoes	1 pound tomatoes
10-15 green olives, halved and stoned	10-15 green olives, halved and stoned
1 oz (30g) raw cane sugar	2½ tablespoonsful raw cane sugar
2 tablespoonsful wine vinegar	2 tablespoonsful wine vinegar
2 tablespoonsful capers	2 tablespoonsful capers
Seaoning to taste	Seasoning to taste
4 hard-boiled eggs *or* 2 oz (55g) almonds or pine nuts (optional)	4 hard-boiled eggs *or* ½ cupful almonds or pine nuts (optional)

1. Dice the aubergines (eggplants), sprinkle lightly with salt, and set aside for an hour. Then rinse with cold water and pat dry.

2. Heat half the oil in a large pan and fry the aubergine (eggplant) cubes until golden, turning them frequently. Drain on paper towels.

3. Chop the onion, celery and tomatoes. Add the remainder of the oil to the pan, and then sauté the onion for a few minutes before stirring in the celery, tomatoes and olives. Simmer until the celery is cooked.

4. Add the sugar, vinegar, capers, seasoning, and the aubergine (eggplant) cubes, and cook gently for 10 minutes more, or until the liquid thickens to become a light sauce. Adjust the seasoning if necessary.

Note: This dish is usually served cold and unadorned, although sliced eggs or nuts are sometimes arranged on top of the vegetables, turning it into a complete meal. It is also amazingly good eaten hot.

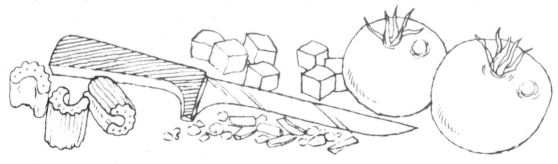

Creamy Peas Pasties

For shortcrust pastry:

Imperial/Metric	American
Pinch of sea salt	Pinch of sea salt
6 oz (170g) plain wholemeal flour	1½ cupsful plain wholewheat flour
3 oz (85g) polyunsaturated margarine	⅓ cupful polyunsaturated margarine
1 tablespoonful cold water	1 tablespoonful cold water

For filling:

Imperial/Metric	American
1 oz (30g) polyunsaturated margarine	2½ tablespoonsful polyunsaturated margarine
1 oz (30g) plain wholemeal flour	¼ cupful plain wholewheat flour
½ pint (285ml) milk	1⅓ cupsful milk
4 oz (115g) peas, fresh *or* frozen	¾ cupful peas, fresh *or* frozen
Seasoning to taste	Seasoning to taste

1.   Add the salt to the flour, then rub in the margarine until the mix resembles fine breadcrumbs.

2.   Gradually blend in the water with a fork until a soft, rather wet dough is formed. Knead the dough a little, then leave it to stand. (As wholemeal flour makes pastry more crumbly, you can make it easier to roll out by first wrapping the dough in cling foil and putting it in the refrigerator for at least 30 minutes.)

3.   Turn the dough onto a floured board, roll it out thinly and use a saucer to cut it into rounds.

4.   Meanwhile, heat the margarine and cook the flour in it gently for a few minutes.

5.   Remove the saucepan from the heat and add the milk, stirring it to prevent lumps forming, then return the sauce to the heat and stir again until it thickens. Season to taste.

6.   Cook and drain the peas and add them to the white sauce.

7.   Place a generous portion of the mixture onto each round of dough, fold them in half and press the edges together.

8.   Place the pasties on a greased baking sheet, and cook for 20-30 minutes at 400°F/200°C (Gas Mark 6).

Chick Pea Purée

Serves 6

Imperial/Metric	American
1 lb (455g) chick peas	2 cupsful garbanzo beans
4 medium onions, finely chopped	4 medium onions, finely chopped
5 cloves garlic, crushed	5 cloves garlic, crushed
¼-½ pint (140-285ml) olive oil	⅔-1⅓ cupsful olive oil
5 tablespoonsful parsley, finely chopped	5 tablespoonsful parsley, finely chopped
2 tablespoonsful dried mint *or*	2 tablespoonsful dried mint *or*
4 tablespoonsful fresh mint	4 tablespoonsful fresh mint
Juice of 2 lemons	Juice of 2 lemons
Sea salt and black pepper	Sea salt and black pepper
Croûtons	Croûtons

1. Boil the chick peas (garbanzo beans) until tender.

2. Drain the chick peas (garbanzo beans) and, when they have cooled, mince them or mash them to a purée.

3. Fry the onions and garlic in a little olive oil until they become transparent.

4. Add the other ingredients and heat through. Use as much olive oil as is needed to give the dish the required consistency. This is largely a matter of personal taste and it will depend on whether the dish is to be used as a dip or as a side dish to the main course.

5. Garnish with croûtons or use as a dip with pitta or wholemeal bread.

Note: There are various other ways of serving this dish. It is excellent hot or cold and it combines particularly well with a crisp, green salad.

Pitta Bread

Imperial/Metric	American
½ lb (225g) wholemeal flour	2 cupsful wholewheat flour
Pinch of sea salt	Pinch of sea salt
¼ oz (7g) fresh yeast	½ tablespoonful fresh yeast
½ teaspoonful raw cane sugar *or* honey	½ teaspoonful raw cane sugar *or* honey
¼ pint (140ml) warm water	⅔ cupful warm water

1.   Sieve together the flour and salt.

2.   Stir the yeast and sugar into the warm water, mixing well until dissolved, then set aside for 15 minutes or so to froth up.

3.   Pour into the flour mixture and knead to make a smooth dough; turn on to a lightly floured board and continue kneading until the dough is very elastic.

4.   Leave the dough to rise, then knead again lightly; divide into 8 portions and roll out to the traditional oval shape about ¼ in. (0.5cm) thick.

5.   Arrange on a greased baking sheet and cook at 400°F/200°C (Gas Mark 6) for about 10 minutes, or until risen. Cool on a wire rack, then, when needed, slit along the side to make a pocket and fill with the ingredients of your choice.

Note: These can also be cooked in a heavy-based pan; lightly grease the pan and put it over a strong heat; when ready, slip pittas one at a time into the pan and then press down with a spatula as it cooks; flip over and cook the other side until just coloured.

Illustrated opposite page 177.

Fruit and Pasta Salad

Imperial/Metric	American
3 oz (85g) wholemeal spaghetti rings	1½ cupsful wholewheat spaghetti rings
2 medium bananas	2 medium bananas
2 oz (55g) dates	½ cupful dates
2 oz (55g) Brazil nuts	½ cupful Brazil nuts
1 large crisp lettuce	1 large crisp lettuce
4 oz (115g) cottage cheese	½ cupful cottage cheese
1 tablespoonful honey (optional)	1 tablespoonful honey (optional)

1.   Cook the spaghetti rings in boiling water; drain, then rinse in cold water.

2.   In a bowl, combine the chopped bananas, dates and nuts with the spaghetti rings.

3.   Arrange the washed lettuce decoratively on a serving dish, and pile the pasta, fruit and nut mixture in the centre. Top with the cheese, mixed — if liked — with honey.

Scotch Eggs

Makes 3

Imperial/Metric	American
1 medium onion, grated	1 medium onion, grated
1 clove garlic, crushed	1 clove garlic, crushed
4 oz (115g) Brazil nuts, ground	¾ cupful Brazil nuts, ground
4 oz (115g) mashed potato	¾ cupful mashed potato
1 tablespoonful tomato purée	1 tablespoonful tomato paste
1 teaspoonful thyme	1 teaspoonful thyme
1 teaspoonful yeast extract	1 teaspoonful yeast extract
Freshly ground black pepper	Freshly ground black pepper
1 tablespoonful vegetable oil	1 tablespoonful vegetable oil
3 eggs, hard-boiled	3 eggs, hard-boiled
1 egg, beaten	1 egg, beaten
4 oz (115g) dry, fine wholemeal breadcrumbs	1½ cupsful dry, fine wholewheat breadcrumbs
Oil for deep-frying	Oil for deep-frying

1.   Mix the onion, garlic, nuts, mashed potato, tomato purée, thyme, yeast extract and seasoning. Add a little oil if the mixture seems a little dry.

2.   Coat the hard-boiled eggs with the nut mix as evenly as possible.

3.   Dip each Scotch Egg in the beaten egg and breadcrumbs and fry in the hot oil until golden brown.

Note: The nutmeat base used here can be varied widely by use of different sorts of nuts, and by varying the flavourings with *Holbrook's* Worcestershire sauce, mushrooms, herbs, leeks, etc. Eggs may be needed to bind the nut mix but should be avoided if possible.

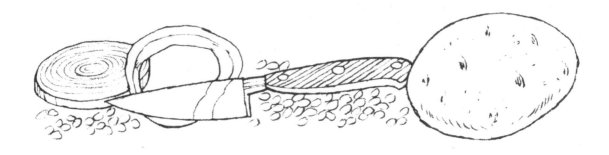

Antipasto Misto

You can use a wide variety of ingredients to make your antipasto misto — in fact, the more the better. Arrange them on one large oval dish, or on individual plates, using the range of colours and shapes to make the food look as appetizing as it is flavoursome. Ingredients to include:

- Pimentos in vegetable oil.
- Cucumber chunks.
- Cherry tomatoes with onion rings.
- Olives, both black and green.
- Small artichokes in vegetable oil.
- Raw broad beans (Windsor beans).
- Raw mushrooms, sliced thinly.
- Chicory.
- Rings of red and green pepper.
- Raw fennel strips.
- Quartered hard-boiled eggs.
- Slices of cheeses such as Mozzarella, Provolone, Gorgonzola, Gruyère.
- Cooked chick peas (garbanzo beans) and kidney beans.

Put a good salad dressing, some mayonnaise, sea salt and a pepper grinder on the table for everyone to add to the antipasto misto as they wish.

Creamy Vegetable Flan

For base:

Imperial/Metric	American
6 oz (170g) rolled oats	1½ cupsful rolled oats
3 oz (85g) polyunsaturated margarine	⅓ cupful polyunsaturated margarine
1 oz (30g) sunflower seeds	¼ cupful sunflower seeds
Seasoning to taste	Seasoning to taste

For filling:

Imperial/Metric	American
Approx. 1 lb (450g) mixed vegetables, e.g. cauliflower florets, carrots, peas, green beans, courgettes, parsnips, etc.	Approx. 1 pound mixed vegetables, e.g. cauliflower florets, carrots, peas, green beans, zucchini, parsnips, etc.
6 oz (170g) cream cheese	¾ cupful cream cheese
Seasoning to taste	Seasoning to taste

1.   Use fingertips to rub the margarine into the oats; add the seeds and seasoning; press mixture down as evenly as possible to line the base and sides of a lightly greased flan dish.

2.   Bake 'blind' for 15 minutes at 400°F/200°C (Gas Mark 6).

3.   Prepare the vegetables by cleaning and chopping them into small even-sized pieces; steam lightly until just tender.

4.   Whilst the vegetables are still warm, stir in the cheese to make a smooth coating.

5.   Spoon the vegetables into the flan case and return to the oven for 10-15 minutes more, until the oat pastry is cooked.

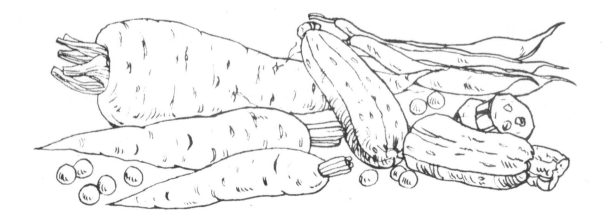

Curried Banana and Rice Salad

Serves 2

Imperial/Metric	American
1 small onion	1 small onion
2 oz (55g) green pepper	½ small green pepper
2 bananas	2 bananas
4 tablespoonsful cooked brown rice	4 tablespoonsful cooked brown rice
2 tablespoonsful unsweetened, desiccated coconut	2 tablespoonsful unsweetened, desiccated coconut
2 teaspoonsful raw cane sugar	2 teaspoonsful raw cane sugar
½ teaspoonful sea salt	½ teaspoonful sea salt
1-2 teaspoonsful curry powder	1-2 teaspoonsful curry powder
2 tablespoonsful lemon juice	2 tablespoonsful lemon juice
4 tablespoonsful sunflower oil	4 tablespoonsful sunflower oil
Chopped fresh parsley	Chopped fresh parsley

1. Peel and chop the onion, de-seed and slice the pepper thinly and peel and dice the bananas.

2. Place the onion, pepper and bananas in a deep serving bowl with the brown rice and coconut.

3. Place the sugar, sea salt, curry powder, lemon juice and oil in a jam jar and shake it well.

4. Pour the dressing over the salad, mix it in carefully and garnish the salad with the parsley. Chill before serving.

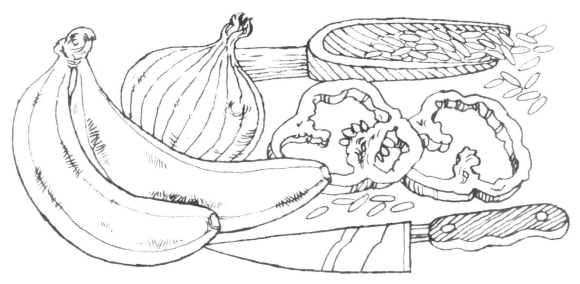

Caesar Salad

Imperial/Metric	American
4 slices wholemeal bread	4 slices wholewheat bread
4 tablespoonsful sunflower oil	4 tablespoonsful sunflower oil
1 clove garlic	1 clove garlic
1 large Cos lettuce	1 large Cos lettuce
1 large endive, chopped	1 large chicory, chopped
1 oz (30g) grated Parmesan cheese	¼ cupful grated Parmesan cheese
2 oz (55g) crumbled blue cheese	½ cupful crumbled blue cheese
3 tablespoonsful lemon juice	3 tablespoonsful lemon juice
½ teaspoonful *Tabasco* sauce	½ teaspoonful *Tabasco* sauce
Mustard to taste	Mustard to taste
¾ teaspoonful sea salt	¾ teaspoonful sea salt
1 raw egg	1 raw egg

1.   Remove the crust from the bread and dice it.

2.   Heat up 2 tablespoonsful of the oil. Chop the garlic clove and add the diced bread and garlic to the oil. Sauté them until lightly browned, then drain them and set to one side.

3.   Tear the lettuce into bite-sized pieces and place it in a salad bowl with the endive (chicory). Sprinkle the Parmesan and blue cheese over the top.

4.   Make a dressing with the remainder of the oil, lemon juice, *Tabasco* sauce, mustard and seasoning in a jar. Shake well and pour the mixture over the salad, tossing it lightly.

5.   Break the egg into the salad and mix it in gently until egg particles disappear.

6.   Add the croûtons and toss the salad lightly again.

Little Asparagus Pizzas

For base:

Imperial/Metric	American
½ lb (225g) self-raising wholemeal flour	2 cupsful self-raising wholewheat flour
2 oz (55g) polyunsaturated margarine	¼ cupful polyunsaturated margarine
Approx. ¼ pint (140ml) milk	⅔ cupful milk
Pinch of sea salt	Pinch of sea salt

For topping:

Imperial/Metric	American
1 oz (30g) polyunsaturated margarine	2½ tablespoonsful polyunsaturated margarine
1 tablespoonful vegetable oil	1 tablespoonful vegetable oil
2 medium onions	2 medium onions
½ lb (225g) ripe tomatoes	8 ounces ripe tomatoes
Approx. 20 cooked asparagus tips	Approx. 20 cooked asparagus tips
1-2 teaspoonsful oregano	1-2 teaspoonsful oregano
Seasoning to taste	Seasoning to taste
6 oz (170g) Emmenthal cheese	1½ cupsful Emmenthal cheese
2 oz (55g) Parmesan cheese	½ cupful Parmesan cheese
Parsley to garnish	Parsley to garnish

1.   Sieve together the flour and salt. Rub the margarine into the dry ingredients to make a crumb-like mixture.

2.   Pour in enough milk to bind the mixture into a soft, manageable dough. Turn onto a floured board and knead lightly.

3.   Divide the dough into 4 and shape into thin rounds. Bake 'blind' at 400°F/200°C (Gas Mark 6) for 5 minutes.

4.   Meanwhile, heat the oil and margarine together, add the sliced onion and cook for a few minutes, then add the skinned, mashed tomatoes.

5.   Cook tomato sauce over moderate heat without a cover so that most of the liquid evaporates, then combine with the drained asparagus tips and heat through for a few minutes more.

6.   Spoon mixture onto the pizza bases, sprinkle with oregano and season well. Top with Emmenthal cheese cut into thin slices, a sprinkling of Parmesan cheese and chopped parsley. Bake at 400°F/200°C (Gas Mark 6) for 15-20 minutes.

Omelette Salad

Imperial/Metric	American
Olive oil for frying	Olive oil for frying
2 eggs	2 eggs
1 tablespoonful milk	1 tablespoonful milk
Sea salt and freshly ground black pepper to taste	Sea salt and freshly ground black pepper to taste
1 dessert apple	1 dessert apple
1 red pepper	1 red pepper
4 oz (115g) mushrooms	2 cupsful mushrooms
2 large cooked potatoes	2 large cooked potatoes
1 lettuce	1 lettuce
12 green stuffed olives, sliced	12 green stuffed olives, sliced
Vinaigrette dressing (page 81) to which 1 tablespoonful dry sherry has been added	Vinaigrette dressing (page 81) to which 1 tablespoonful dry sherry has been added
1 oz (30g) flaked almonds	¼ cupful slivered almonds

1.   Make the omelette by heating the oil in an omelette pan; mix the eggs, milk, salt and pepper and pour into pan. Fry gently until the mixture is set.

2.   Turn the omelette out and allow to cool. Then cut into small squares.

3.   Core and slice the apple, then de-seed the pepper and cut into strips. Wash and slice the mushrooms thinly, dice the potatoes and wash and separate the lettuce. Dry thoroughly.

4.   Arrange the lettuce leaves around a serving bowl and place the mushrooms, peppers, potatoes, olives, apple and omelette on top. Pour over the French dressing and sprinkle with flaked (slivered) almonds.

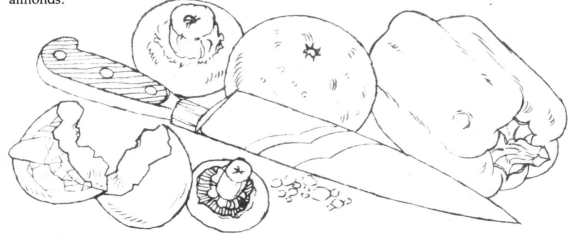

Tabbouleh

Serves 6

Imperial/Metric   *American*

Imperial/Metric	American
¾ lb (340g) burghul	2⅓ cupsful burghul
1 medium onion, very finely chopped	1 medium onion, very finely chopped
4 oz (115g) parsley, finely chopped	4 cupsful parsley, finely chopped
2 oz (55g) mint, finely chopped	2 cupsful mint, finely chopped
2 teaspoonsful sea salt	2 teaspoonsful sea salt
5 tablespoonsful olive oil	5 tablespoonsful olive oil
Juice of 2 lemons	Juice of 2 lemons
Seasoning	Seasoning
Vine or lettuce leaves	Vine or lettuce leaves
Lemon wedges	Lemon wedges
6 firm tomatoes	6 firm tomatoes
12 black olives	12 black olives

1.   Soak the burghul in water for about 30 minutes and drain well.

2.   Mix the burghul with the onion, parsley, mint, salt, olive oil and lemon juice. If you wish to season your tabbouleh, use freshly ground black pepper, cayenne pepper or cinnamon.

3.   Serve on a bed of vine or lettuce leaves. Garnish the salad attractively with lemon wedges, tomato wedges, and black olives.

Illustrated opposite page 80.

Walnut Balls

For 6

Imperial/Metric	American
6 oz (170g) walnuts, ground	1½ cupsful English walnuts, ground
3 oz (85g) wholemeal breadcrumbs	1½ cupsful wholewheat breadcrumbs
4 oz (115g) Cheddar, grated	1 cupful Cheddar, grated
1 medium onion, grated	1 medium onion, grated
Freshly ground black pepper	Freshly ground black pepper
Sea salt	Sea salt
2 tablespoonsful parsley	2 tablespoonsful parsley
1 tin red peppers, diced	1 can red peppers, diced
1 egg, beaten	1 egg, beaten
Milk (if required)	Milk (if required)

1.   Mix the walnuts, breadcrumbs, cheese and onion in a bowl.

2.   Season with pepper and salt and add the parsley and red peppers.

3.   Finally, add the egg and combine well with the other ingredients. If the mixture is too dry, add a little milk.

4.   Form the mixture into balls and arrange in a well-greased baking dish.

5.   Bake in a moderate oven at 350°F/180°C (Gas Mark 4) for about 25 minutes until brown.

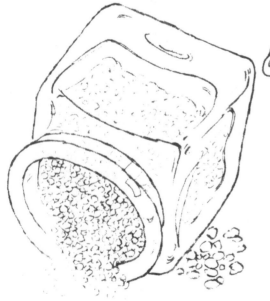

Opposite: An Italian meal with a choice of dishes — Spinach and Ricotta Gnocci (page 62) with Breadsticks (page 164) or Cooked-in-the-Pan Pizza Margherita (page 44).

Overleaf: Christmas with a difference! Serve Wheat Berry Stew (page 112) with Potato Balls (page 68) and Brussels Sprouts with Chestnuts (page 21), followed by Mincemeat and Apple Crumble (page 171).

French Vegetable Salad

Serves 6

Imperial/Metric	American
1 lb (455g) new potatoes	1 pound new potatoes
1 lb (455g) carrots, scraped	1 pound carrots, scraped
Sea salt	Sea salt
½ lb (225g) fresh green beans	½ pound fresh green beans
½ lb (225g) peas	1⅓ cupsful peas
1 cauliflower	1 cauliflower
1 large cucumber	1 large cucumber
Vinaigrette dressing (page 81)	Vinaigrette dressing (page 81)
Chopped parsley	Chopped parsley
4 tablespoonsful capers	4 tablespoonsful capers

1. Cook the potatoes and carrots in boiling salted water until tender.

2. Put the potatoes into cold water before peeling them carefully. Dice the potatoes and carrots into small cubes.

3. Cook the beans and peas in boiling water for a short time.

4. Cook the cauliflower florets in the same way in boiling water for a short time. They should still be crisp.

5. Peel the cucumber thinly and dice it.

6. Arrange the vegetables attractively on a tray and season well with vinaigrette dressing.

7. Chill well and garnish with parsley and capers.

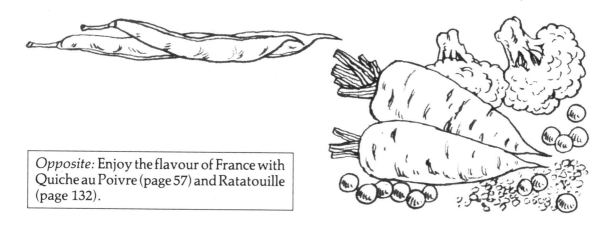

Opposite: Enjoy the flavour of France with Quiche au Poivre (page 57) and Ratatouille (page 132).

Red and Green Risotto

Imperial/Metric	American
4 tablespoonsful vegetable oil	⅓ cupful vegetable oil
1 small onion	1 small onion
2 small red peppers	2 small red peppers
2 small green peppers	2 small green peppers
2 sticks of celery	2 stalks of celery
2 tomatoes	2 tomatoes
Basil	Basil
Seasoning to taste	Seasoning to taste
10 oz (285g) brown rice	1¼ cupful brown rice
1½ pints (¾ litre) vegetable stock	3¾ cupful vegetable stock
1 oz (30g) polyunsaturated margarine *or* butter	2½ tablespoonsful polyunsaturated margarine *or* butter
1 oz (30g) pistachio nuts	¼ cupful pistachio nuts

1.   Heat the oil in a saucepan, slice the onion, dice the peppers, chop the celery, and add them all to the oil. Stir well, then cover and cook on a medium heat for 15 minutes, checking that the mixture does not get too dry (if it does, add a tiny drop of water).

2.   Stir in the coarsely chopped tomatoes, basil and seasoning and the rice; cook a minute more. Add the vegetable stock, bring to the boil then cover and simmer for 30 minutes, or until the rice is cooked.

3.   Transfer the risotto to a serving dish, top with knobs of butter and sprinkling of nuts.

Note: Pistachios look especially good with this dish, but if you cannot find (or afford) them, use whatever nuts you have handy.

Aubergine and Pepper 'Caviare'

Serves 6

Imperial/Metric	American
3 medium aubergines	3 medium eggplants
3 peppers, preferably red	3 peppers, preferably red
3 cloves garlic, crushed	3 cloves garlic, crushed
Up to 6 tablespoonsful olive oil	Up to ½ cupful olive oil
Sea salt and freshly ground black pepper	Sea salt and freshly ground black pepper
2 tablespoonsful lemon juice	2 tablespoonsful lemon juice
2 tablespoonsful peanut butter *or* tahini	2 tablespoonsful peanut butter *or* tahini

1.   Put the aubergines (eggplants) and peppers into a very hot oven at 450°F/230°C (Gas Mark 8) and cook until they are tender and the skin is blackening.

2.   Skin them as best you can and blend well with all the other ingredients except the peanut butter or tahini.

3.   Stir in the peanut butter or tahini until you have the desired consistency.

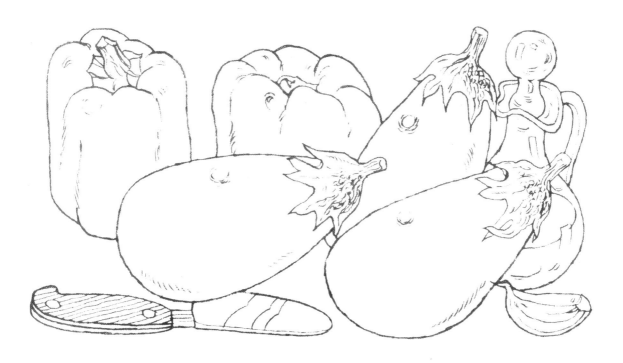

Eggless Egg Salad

Imperial/Metric	American
1½ lb (680g) tofu, pressed for 30 minutes and mashed with a fork	3 cupsful tofu, pressed for 30 minutes and mashed with a fork
1 stick celery, finely chopped	1 stalk celery, finely chopped
1 small onion, or 3-4 spring onions, chopped	1 small onion or 3-4 scallions, chopped
1 tablespoonful soya sauce	1 tablespoonful soy sauce
4 fl oz (120ml) mayonnaise	½ cupful mayonnaise
1 teaspoonful turmeric	1 teaspoonful turmeric

1. Mix all the ingredients together with a fork.

Winter Warmers

Noodles with Walnut Sauce

Imperial/Metric	American
2 oz (55g) walnuts	½ cupful English walnuts
Parsley	Parsley
Seasoning to taste	Seasoning to taste
2 oz (55g) polyunsaturated margarine	¼ cupful polyunsaturated margarine
2 tablespoonsful vegetable oil	2 tablespoonsful vegetable oil
1 oz (30g) fine wholemeal breadcrumbs	½ cupful fine wholewheat breadcrumbs
2 tablespoonsful creamy milk	2 tablespoonsful creamy milk
½ lb (225g) wholemeal noodles	8 ounces wholewheat noodles

1. Remove the skins from the walnuts if preferred.

2. Pound or grind the nuts to make a paste; add the finely chopped parsley and seasoning and mix well.

3. Use a wooden spoon to mix in the margarine, oil and crumbs; continue blending until you have a thick, creamy sauce.

4. Stir in the milk and adjust the seasoning. (If the sauce is too thick, add oil or cream to adjust the consistency.)

5. Cook the noodles in boiling water until tender; drain and serve with the walnut sauce, and a garnish of parsley.

Serves 4 – 332 cals per serving.

Pepper and Sunflower Seed Pie

Imperial/Metric	American
4 medium potatoes *560g*	4 medium potatoes
2 large peppers	2 large peppers
1 large onion	1 large onion
4 oz (115g) sunflower seeds	1 cupful sunflower seeds
¼ pint (140ml) vegetable stock	⅔ cupful vegetable stock
1 teaspoonful yeast extract	1 teaspoonful yeast extract
Seasoning to taste	Seasoning to taste

(handwritten margin notes: 500, 50, 50, 625, 50, 50)

1. Peel the potatoes and slice thinly; chop the peppers and onion.

2. Place a layer of potatoes in a pie dish, cover with some chopped pepper and onion, sprinkle with some sunflower seeds.

3. Repeat until all the ingredients are used, finishing with a layer of potatoes. Pour on the stock in which the yeast extract has been dissolved. Season. Cover with lid or silver foil.

4. Bake at 300°F/150°C (Gas Mark 2) for 1 hour, or until cooked.

Cauliflower Oat Crumble

For topping:

Imperial/Metric	American
3 oz (85g) rolled oats	¾ cupful rolled oats
2 oz (55g) grated Cheddar cheese	½ cupful grated Cheddar cheese
2 oz (55g) polyunsaturated margarine *or* butter	¼ cupful polyunsaturated margarine *or* butter

For base:

Imperial/Metric	American
1 medium cauliflower	1 medium cauliflower
4 oz (115g) grated Cheddar cheese	1 cupful grated Cheddar cheese
2 oz (55g) wheatgerm	½ cupful wheatgerm
Good pinch of nutmeg	Good pinch of nutmeg
Seasoning to taste	Seasoning to taste

1.   Put the oats into a bowl with the finely grated cheese, then use your fingertips to rub in the margarine to make a very coarse crumble.

2.   Break the cauliflower into florets and steam or boil in the minimum amount of water for 10 minutes, or until tender. Drain well.

3.   Mash the cauliflower to make a soft, smooth mixture — if it seems very dry, add a little of the water in which it was cooked. Stir in the grated cheese, wheatgerm, nutmeg and seasoning.

4.   Transfer the mixture to a lightly greased ovenproof dish, then spread the prepared crumble over the top and press it down lightly. Bake at 375°F/190°C (Gas Mark 5) for 20 minutes, or until the topping is lightly browned.

Buckwheat with Miso

Imperial/Metric	American
6 oz (170g) buckwheat	¾ cupful buckwheat
2 large onions	2 large onions
1 large green pepper	1 large green pepper
1 tablespoonful vegetable oil	1 tablespoonful vegetable oil
Approx. 1 teaspoonful miso	Approx. 1 teaspoonful miso
2 oz (55g) peanuts	½ cupful peanuts
2 oz (55g) fresh beansprouts	1 cupful fresh beansprouts

1.   Dry-roast the buckwheat until beginning to brown.

2.   Lightly sauté the sliced onions and pepper in the oil for a few minutes.

3.   Add the buckwheat and cook for 1 minute more, then pour on enough water to cover the ingredients and bring to the boil.

4.   Cover and cook gently until all the ingredients are tender.

5.   When almost ready to eat, take a little of the liquid from the saucepan and mix it with the miso. Return it to the pan with the peanuts and beansprouts for a few minutes more.

Aubergine Cheese Rolls

Rolls:

Imperial/Metric	American
4 medium aubergines	4 medium eggplants
Sea salt	Sea salt
Approx. 2 oz (55g) wholemeal flour	Approx. ½ cupful wholewheat flour
Vegetable oil for frying	Vegetable oil for frying
½ lb (225g) Ricotta cheese	1 cupful Ricotta cheese

Sauce:

Imperial/Metric	American
2 oz (55g) polyunsaturated margarine *or* butter	¼ cupful polyunsaturated margarine *or* butter
2 oz (55g) plain wholemeal flour	½ cupful plain wholewheat flour
1 pint (570ml) milk	2½ cupsful milk
Seasoning to taste	Seasoning to taste
1 oz (30g) grated Parmesan cheese	¼ cupful grated Parmesan cheese
2 egg yolks	2 egg yolks

1.   Wash the aubergines (eggplants), trim the bases, then cut lengthways into very thin slices. Lay them on a plate, sprinkle with salt, and leave for 30 minutes. Rinse thoroughly in cold water, then pat the slices with paper towels to dry.

2.   Coat them evenly in flour and fry quickly in vegetable oil until lightly browned on each side. Drain well on paper towels and leave to cool.

3.   Roll each of the slices up, placing a small amount of the cheese in the centre of each roll. Arrange them close together in an ovenproof dish — if you like you can secure the rolls with a skewer or toothpick, but it should not really be necessary.

4.   To make the béchamel sauce, melt the margarine and sauté the flour in it for a few minutes on a low heat. Stir in the milk, and continue stirring as it comes to the boil.

5.   When the sauce is thick and completely smooth remove it from the heat and cool slightly before adding the seasoning, grated cheese and egg yolks. Mix well. Pour the sauce over the aubergine (eggplant) rolls making sure it is evenly distributed.

6.   Bake at 375°F/190°C (Gas Mark 5) for about 10 minutes, or until heated through.

Note: This is a very rich dish so the amounts given here could well be enough for 6 servings. If you cannot obtain Ricotta cheese, you could just omit it and still produce a tasty dish. A tomato sauce can be used instead of the béchamel.

Bean Enchiladas

For tortillas:

Imperial/Metric	American
½ lb (225g) maize flour	1½ cupsful cornmeal
Sea salt to taste	Sea salt to taste
Approx. ½ pint (285ml) warm water	1⅓ cupsful warm water

For filling:

Imperial/Metric	American
½ lb (225g) cooked mixed beans	1 cupful cooked mixed beans
2 tablespoonsful vegetable oil	2 tablespoonsful vegetable oil
1 onion	1 onion
½-1 clove garlic, crushed	½-1 clove garlic, crushed
4 ripe tomatoes	4 ripe tomatoes
2 tablespoonsful tomato purée	2 tablespoonsful tomato paste
½-1 tablespoonful chilli powder	½-1 tablespoonful chilli powder
1 teaspoonful paprika	1 teaspoonful paprika
Seasoning to taste	Seasoning to taste
1 small carton soured cream	1 small carton soured cream

1.   Sift together the maize flour (cornflour) and salt; gradually stir in enough water to make a dough and knead briefly.

2.   Divide into 12 portions and roll out on a floured surface, to make them into 6 in. (15cm) circles.

3.   Cook the tortillas one at a time in a skillet or heavy-based pan. Traditionally they are made without oil, and are simply cooked over a medium heat for a few minutes on each side, until lightly browned. If you prefer, you can shallow-fry them in a minimum amount of oil.

4.   Whilst still warm, wrap each one around some of the bean mixture. Arrange close together in a heatproof dish with the join facing downwards.

5.   In a saucepan, heat the oil and lightly sauté the sliced onion with the garlic for 10 minutes; add the chopped tomatoes, purée, chilli powder, paprika and seasoning.

6.   Bring the sauce to the boil, then lower the heat, cover and simmer until a thick paste is formed. Adjust seasoning.

7.   Pour sauce evenly over the tortillas, spoon the soured cream over the top. Bake at 350°F/180°C (Gas Mark 4) for 10-15 minutes, or until heated through.

Sweetcorn, Bean and Barley Soup

Imperial/Metric	American
2 tablespoonsful vegetable oil	2 tablespoonsful vegetable oil
1-2 cloves garlic, crushed	1-2 cloves garlic, crushed
4 oz (115g) sweetcorn kernels, fresh *or* frozen	½ cupful sweetcorn kernels, fresh *or* frozen
4 oz (115g) borlotti beans, soaked overnight	½ cupful borlotti beans, soaked overnight
4 oz (115g) pearl *or* pot barley, soaked overnight	½ cupful pearl *or* pot barley, soaked overnight
2 pints (1 litre) vegetable stock	5 cupsful vegetable stock
1 large leek	1 large leek
Seasoning to taste	Seasoning to taste
Parsley	Parsley

1. Heat the oil and fry the garlic gently till it begins to colour.

2. Add the sweetcorn (defrost and drain first if using the frozen kind), plus the drained beans, barley, and the vegetable stock. Bring to the boil, then cook gently for 50 minutes.

3. Clean the leek, chop coarsely, and add to the saucepan, and continue cooking for about 10 minutes more, or until all the ingredients are tender.

4. Just before serving, season the soup to taste, and stir in a generous amount of chopped parsley. Serve with Black Peasant Bread (opposite).

Illustrated opposite page 33.

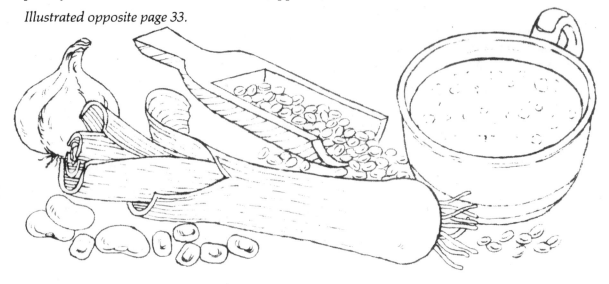

Black Peasant Bread

Imperial/Metric	American
¾ pint (425ml) hot water	2 cupsful hot water
4 tablespoonsful molasses	⅓ cupful molasses
¾ oz (20g) dried yeast	1½ tablespoonsful dried yeast
¼ pint (140ml) warm water	⅔ cupful warm water
1 teaspoonful raw cane sugar	1 teaspoonful raw cane sugar
1½ lb (680g) rye flour	6 cupsful rye flour
1 teaspoonful sea salt	1 teaspoonful sea salt
3 tablespoonsful vegetable oil	3 tablespoonsful vegetable oil

1. Put the hot water into a bowl and add the molasses. Mix well.

2. Dissolve the yeast in the warm water and add the sugar. Let it stand in a warm place for about 15 minutes.

3. Stir the yeast and molasses into the rye flour and add the salt and oil.

4. Put the dough into a greased bowl and cover. Leave in a warm place for about 15 minutes.

5. Knead the dough for about 10 minutes.

6. Put the dough back into the greased bowl and leave in a warm place for about 90 minutes until double the original size.

7. Form into one large loaf or two smaller loaves. Make the loaves as high as possible as they will spread out and flatten while baking.

8. Place on a piece of greaseproof paper and allow to rise for 30 minutes.

9. Bake for 40 minutes at 400°F/200°C (Gas Mark 6).

Illustrated opposite page 161.

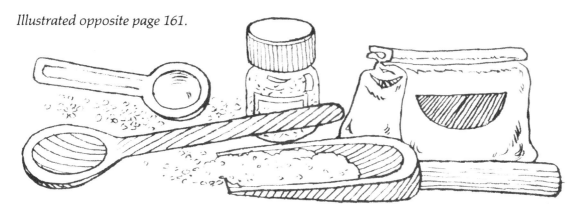

Polenta

Imperial/Metric	American
1¾ pints (1 litre) water	4 cupsful water
½ lb (225g) Polenta (maize flour)	2 cupsful Polenta (cornmeal)
Sea salt	Sea salt
2 oz (55g) polyunsaturated margarine	¼ cupful polyunsaturated margarine
2 oz (55g) Parmesan, grated	½ cupful Parmesan, grated
1 egg, beaten	1 egg, beaten
Dry, fine wholemeal breadcrumbs	Dry, fine wholewheat breadcrumbs
Olive oil for frying	Olive oil for frying

1.   Bring the water to the boil in a large saucepan.

2.   Pour in the Polenta slowly, stirring constantly to avoid lumps. Use a long wooden spoon to stir the Polenta as it has a tendency to 'spit' while it is being cooked.

3.   Add the salt and margarine.

4.   Cook on a low heat for 20 minutes until it is thick but smooth and soft. When it is ready it should come away from the sides of the pan as you stir.

5.   Add the Parmesan cheese.

6.   Pour the Polenta into a greased tin which is at least 2 in. (5cm) deep.

7.   Allow the Polenta to cool and set — an hour should be sufficient.

8.   When the Polenta is solid, cut it into small squares, or use a rinsed inverted glass to make rounds.

9.   Dip each piece into beaten egg and roll in breadcrumbs.

10.   Fry in olive oil until golden brown all over. Drain on kitchen paper.

Shepherd's Pie

Imperial/Metric	American
6 oz (170g) lentils, split peas *or* soya minced 'meat', pre-soaked	Approx. 1 cupful lentils, split peas *or* soy minced 'meat', pre-soaked
1 lb (455g) potatoes	1 pound potatoes
1 tablespoonful vegetable oil	1 tablespoonful vegetable oil
1 onion, chopped	1 onion, chopped
2 tablespoonsful tomato purée	2 tablespoonsful tomato paste
1 tablespoonful marjoram	1 tablespoonful marjoram
Seasoning to taste	Seasoning to taste
Polyunsaturated margarine *or* butter (optional)	Polyunsaturated margarine *or* butter (optional)

1.   Cook the lentils, peas or soya minced 'meat' in plenty of water until just tender.

2.   Meanwhile, peel and cube the potatoes and steam them until soft.

3.   In a frying pan (skillet), heat the oil and lightly sauté the onion.

4.   Add the drained lentils, peas or soya 'meat' together with the tomato purée, marjoram and seasoning. Cook for just a few minutes, stirring well so that the flavours mingle.

5.   Spread the drained mixture across the base of a shallow ovenproof dish.

6.   Mash the potatoes with a little sea salt and freshly ground black pepper, and spread them over the other ingredients. Use a fork to smooth the top and make a decorative pattern — for a more golden top, add a few knobs of margarine or butter.

7.   If all the ingredients are hot, you can just heat the dish under the grill for a few minutes, or until the potatoes begin to colour. If cold, put the dish in the oven at 400°F/200°C (Gas Mark 6) for 10 minutes, or until heated through.

Note: A much quicker way to make this dish, of course, is to use leftovers. Any protein and vegetable mix can be used as the base — just add a few herbs and some yeast extract or tomato purée if it needs more flavour (and if you cook extra potatoes, you'll always have some handy for the topping).

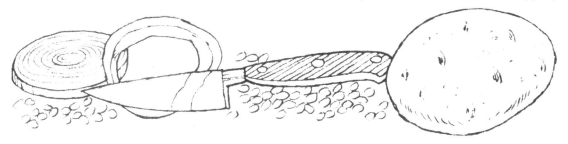

Mutter Pilau (with peas)

Imperial/Metric	American
2 onions, finely sliced	2 onions, finely sliced
4 oz (115g) ghee *or* vegetable fat	½ cupful ghee *or* vegetable fat
Seeds of 5 cardamoms	Seeds of 5 cardamoms
5 × 1 in. (2.5cm) sticks of cinnamon	5 × 1 inch (2.5cm) sticks of cinnamon
5 black peppercorns	5 black peppercorns
5 cloves	5 cloves
½ lb (225g) brown rice	1 cupful brown rice
1½ lb (680g) fresh peas	1½ pounds fresh peas
Sea salt to taste	Sea salt to taste
1 tomato to garnish	1 tomato to garnish

1.   Fry the onions until golden brown in the fat; add the cardamoms, cinnamon, peppercorns and cloves and brown them.

2.   Add the rice and fry it for 10 minutes. Pour 2 pints (1 litre) of boiling water into the pan, add the peas, and cook until the rice is tender and the water has evaporated. Add salt to taste.

3.   Turn the rice out into a dish and garnish it with thin slices of tomato. Serve with pickle, chutney and yogurt.

Note: Broad beans (Windsor beans) or sweetcorn may be used instead of peas.

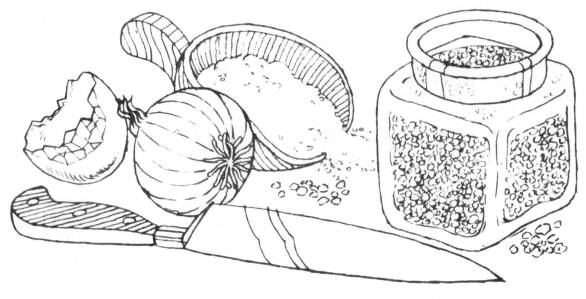

Lasagne with Red Peppers

Imperial/Metric	American
6 oz (170g) wholemeal lasagne	6 ounces wholewheat lasagne
2 tablespoonsful vegetable oil	2 tablespoonsful vegetable oil
2 medium onions	2 medium onions
2 medium red peppers	2 medium red peppers
2 oz (55g) walnut pieces	½ cupful English walnut pieces
3 medium tomatoes	3 medium tomatoes
1 teaspoonful basil	1 teaspoonful basil
Seasoning to taste	Seasoning to taste
10 black olives	10 black olives
2 eggs	2 eggs
¾ pint (425ml) plain yogurt	2 cupsful natural yogurt
2 oz (55g) Cheddar cheese, grated	½ cupful Cheddar cheese, grated

1.   Cook the lasagne; drain, then rinse thoroughly in cold water.

2.   Heat the vegetable oil and gently sauté the sliced onions and peppers until they start to soften.

3.   Add the walnuts and cook a few minutes more.

4.   Chop the tomatoes and add to the pan with the basil and seasoning; simmer for 5 minutes, stirring often.

5.   Stone and halve the olives; stir into the vegetables.

6.   Layer half the lasagne in a greased heatproof dish; top with the vegetable nut mixture; cover with the rest of the lasagne.

7.   Beat the eggs lightly; add to the yogurt; season well.

8.   Pour the sauce over the lasagne, tipping the dish so that it runs down between the ingredients.

9.   Sprinkle with the grated cheese.

10.   Bake at 400°F/200°C (Gas Mark 6) for 30-40 minutes, or until set.

Illustrated opposite page 112.

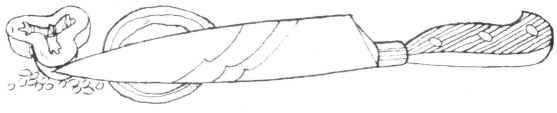

Wheat Berry Stew

Imperial/Metric	American
2 tablespoonsful vegetable oil	2 tablespoonsful vegetable oil
½ lb (225g) wheat berries, soaked overnight	1 cupful wheat berries, soaked overnight
2 large onions	2 large onions
2 large carrots	2 large carrots
2 large green peppers	2 large green peppers
4 oz (115g) small red lentils	½ cupful small red lentils
1 teaspoonful basil	1 teaspoonful basil
Seasoning to taste	Seasoning to taste

1.   Heat the oil and gently sauté the drained berries and chopped vegetables, stirring frequently.

2.   Add the lentils and cook for a minute or two longer.

3.   Add the seasoning and herbs, cover with boiling water, then put a lid on the pan and simmer gently until the berries are tender. (You may need to add a drop more water during the cooking process.)

Illustrated between pages 96 and 97.

Opposite: Lasagne with Red Peppers (page 111) is a satisfying dish for a Winter's evening.

Dhall Fritters

Imperial/Metric	American
½ lb (225g) lentils	1 cupful lentils
4 onions, sliced	4 onions, sliced
1 egg	1 egg
1 teaspoonful each cumin and turmeric	1 teaspoonful each cumin and turmeric
Seeds of 2 cardamoms	Seeds of 2 cardamoms
2 cloves garlic, crushed	2 cloves garlic, crushed
Just over ⅓ pint (200ml) natural yogurt	1 cupful natural yogurt
1 dried red chilli, crushed	1 dried red chilli, crushed
½ green chilli, sliced	½ green chilli, sliced
Sea salt to taste	Sea salt to taste
Vegetable fat for frying	Vegetable fat for frying

1. Cover the lentils with water and soak them overnight.

2. Drain and grind them, mixing in all the ingredients to make a thick batter.

3. Drop teaspoonsful of the batter into the hot vegetable fat, which should be deep enough to cover the fritters.

4. Remove the fritters when they have risen to the surface and are cooked (1-2 minutes).

Variation: 1 teaspoonful of cinnamon may be used instead of cardamom.

Opposite: A warming Indian meal for a Winter dinner party. Try Mixed Vegetable Curry (page 18) with Bagathed Khichiri (page 73) and Cucumber Raita (page 76).

Cheesy Leek Pancakes

For batter:

Imperial/Metric	American
4 oz (115g) plain wholemeal flour	1 cupful plain wholewheat flour
1 egg	1 egg
½ pint (285ml) milk, *or* half milk and half water	1⅓ cupsful milk, *or* half milk and half water
Pinch of sea salt	Pinch of sea salt

For filling:

Imperial/Metric	American
1 lb (455g) leeks	1 pound of leeks
1 oz (30g) polyunsaturated margarine	2½ tablespoonsful polyunsaturated margarine
1 oz (30g) plain wholemeal flour	¼ cupful plain wholewheat flour
½ pint (285ml) milk	1⅓ cupsful milk
4 oz (115g) cottage *or* Quark cheese	½ cupful cottage *or* Quark cheese
Pinch of paprika	Pinch of paprika
Seasoning to taste	Seasoning to taste
2 oz (55g) Cheddar cheese	½ cupful Cheddar cheese

1. Sieve together the flour and salt, then add the egg and stir briefly.

2. Gradually pour in the liquid, stirring continually to blend in the flour and remove lumps, and continue beating until you have a smooth creamy batter. Leave in the fridge for at least 30 minutes, then beat again before using.

3. Clean, chop and steam the leeks, or cook in the minimum of water.

4. Meanwhile, make a white sauce; heat the margarine until melted, stir in the flour and then the milk, and continue stirring until the sauce thickens.

5. Sieve or mash the cottage cheese and mix into the sauce with the drained leeks, paprika and seasoning.

6. Cook the pancakes, keeping them warm whilst you use up all the batter.

7. Stuff each one with some of the mixture, fold, and place neatly in a heatproof dish. Sprinkle with the grated Cheddar and pop under the grill for 1 minute.

Gratin Savoyard

Serves 6

Imperial/Metric	American
1 pint (570ml) single cream	2½ cupsful light cream
½ lb (225g) Gruyère cheese, grated	2 cupsful Gruyère cheese, grated
1 tablespoonful rosemary, finely chopped	1 tablespoonful rosemary, finely chopped
Seasoning	Seasoning
2 lb (1.15 kilos) new potatoes, cleaned and thinly sliced	2 pounds new potatoes, cleaned and thinly sliced
6 oz (170g) wholemeal breadcrumbs	3 cupsful wholewheat breadcrumbs
2 oz (55g) butter	¼ cupful butter

1. Mix together the cream, cheese and rosemary and seasoning.

2. Butter a large casserole and arrange in it layers of potatoes followed by the cream mixture, finishing with the cream mixture on the top.

3. Sprinkle with the breadcrumbs, dot with butter and cover.

4. Cook at 350°F/180°C (Gas Mark 4) for 2 hours until the potatoes are tender.

Note: You may prefer to speed up the cooking of this delicious dish by boiling the potatoes until just tender before peeling and slicing. The dish can then be cooked in half the time in the oven.

Goulash

Serves 6

Imperial/Metric	American
½ lb (225g) tvp, rehydrated in red wine	2 cupsful tvp, rehydrated in red wine
4 oz (115g) butter	½ cupful butter
6 cloves garlic, crushed	6 cloves garlic, crushed
6 medium onions, thinly sliced	6 medium onions, thinly sliced
8 tinned red peppers, roughly chopped	8 canned red peppers, roughly chopped
2 × 14 oz (395g) tins tomatoes	2 medium cans tomatoes
2 tablespoonsful tomato purée	2 tablespoonsful tomato paste
Sea salt	Sea salt
2 teaspoonsful paprika	2 teaspoonsful paprika

1. Drain off the tvp and reserve any excess liquid.

2. Melt half the butter and fry the tvp and garlic for about 10 minutes.

3. Fry the onions in the rest of the butter until they become transparent.

4. Add the peppers, tomatoes, reserved liquid and tomato purée to the onions and season with the sea salt and paprika.

5. Add the tvp and cook gently for about 40 minutes or until the tvp is tender.

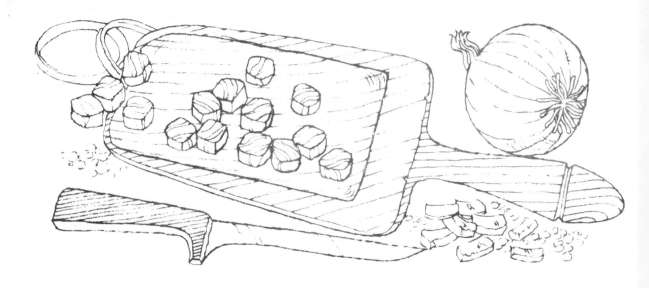

Rice Croquettes

Imperial/Metric	American
1 chopped onion	1 chopped onion
2 cloves garlic, crushed	2 cloves garlic, crushed
1 lb 2 oz (500g) short-grain brown rice	3¾ cupful cooked short-grain brown rice
2 oz (55g) grated Cheddar cheese	½ cupful grated Cheddar cheese
2 tablespoonsful wholemeal flour	2 tablespoonsful wholewheat flour
1 beaten egg	1 beaten egg
Wholemeal breadcrumbs or bran	Wholewheat breadcrumbs or bran

1. Sauté the onion and garlic until golden, then mix with the cooked rice and grated cheese.

2. Mix with flour to a consistency which can be shaped into small patties.

3. Dip into beaten egg, dredge in breadcrumbs or bran (or a mixture of the two).

4. Bake at 350°F/180°C (Gas Mark 4) for 30 minutes and serve with bechamel or tamari soya sauce.

Tahini Vegetable Flan

For pastry:

Imperial/Metric	American
Pastry to line an 8 in. (20cm) flan dish (see page 61)	Pastry to line an 8 inch flan dish (see page 61)
2 tablespoonsful sesame seeds	2 tablespoonsful sesame seeds

For filling:

Imperial/Metric	American
2 oz (55g) peas, fresh *or* frozen	⅓ cupful peas, fresh *or* frozen
4 large carrots	4 large carrots
2 large onions	2 large onions
1 small cabbage	1 small cabbage
2 large sticks celery	2 large stalks celery
2 tablespoonsful vegetable oil	2 tablespoonsful vegetable oil
1-2 teaspoonsful mixed herbs	1-2 teaspoonsful mixed herbs
Soya sauce	Soy sauce
Seasoning to taste	Seasoning to taste
3 tablespoonsful tahini	3 tablespoonsful tahini

1.   Add sesame seeds to pastry dough; roll out and line a flan dish; bake 'blind' for 15 minutes at 400°F/200°C (Gas Mark 6).

2.   Cook the peas in a little water, then drain well.

3.   Peel and slice the carrots and onions; shred the washed cabbage; chop up the celery.

4.   Heat the oil and stir-fry the prepared vegetables on a medium heat for about 5 minutes, making sure they do not burn.

5.   Add the herbs and a sprinkling of soya sauce and turn the heat low; cover the pan and cook the vegetables for 10 minutes more. (You may need to add a spoonful of water.)

6.   Stir in the peas and seasoning; add the tahini and blend well until the vegetables are covered in a thick creamy sauce.

7.   Pour into the flan case and bake at 350°F/180°C (Gas Mark 4) for 15 minutes, or until pastry is cooked. Serve hot.

Potato Pizza

For base

Imperial/Metric	American
½ teaspoonful dried yeast	½ teaspoonful dried yeast
¼ pint (140ml) warm water	⅔ cupful warm water
1 tablespoonful vegetable oil	1 tablespoonful vegetable oil
½ lb (225g) plain wholemeal flour	2 cupsful plain wholewheat flour

For topping:

Imperial/Metric	American
8 small potatoes, preferably new	8 small potatoes, preferably new
1 tablespoonful vegetable oil	1 tablespoonful vegetable oil
2 large onions	2 large onions
1 clove garlic, crushed	1 clove garlic, crushed
1 lb (455g) ripe tomatoes	1 pound ripe tomatoes
1 tablespoonful basil *or* oregano	1 tablespoonful basil *or* oregano
Seasoning to taste	Seasoning to taste
2 oz (55g) grated Parmesan cheese	½ cupful grated Parmesan cheese
10 olives	10 olives
Parsley to garnish	Parsley to garnish

1. Sprinkle the yeast onto the warm water, stir, and set aside until the mixture bubbles.

2. Stir in the oil, then gradually add the liquid to the sifted flour.

3. When this becomes difficult, turn the dough onto a floured board and knead for 5-10 minutes to make a soft, elastic dough.

4. Divide mixture into two and roll out immediately to make two thin circles.

5. Steam the potatoes until just tender, cool slightly, then slice as thinly as possible and arrange attractively on pizza dough.

6. Heat the vegetable oil and lightly sauté the sliced onion and garlic for 3 minutes. Wash and chop the tomatoes and add to the onion with herbs and seasoning; cook until mixture is thick, and most of the liquid has dried up.

7. Pour sauce over potatoes, spreading it evenly. Sprinkle with cheese, decorate with halved, stoned olives and bake at 400°F/200°C (Gas Mark 6) for 20-25 minutes. Garnish with fresh, chopped parsley. Serve cut into slices.

Pot-Au-Feu

Imperial/Metric	American
½ lb (225g) beef-flavoured soya 'meat' chunks	2 cupsful beef-flavoured soy 'meat' chunks
1 tablespoonful vegetable oil	1 tablespoonful vegetable oil
3 leeks	3 leeks
1 small cauliflower	1 small cauliflower
2 oz (55g) brown rice	¼ cupful brown rice
4 oz (115g) fresh *or* frozen peas	⅔ cupful fresh *or* frozen peas
Pinch of cayenne pepper and rosemary	Pinch of cayenne pepper and rosemary
2 bay leaves	2 bay leaves
Seasoning to taste	Seasoning to taste
2 large tomatoes	2 large tomatoes

1. Hydrate the soya 'meat' in boiling water to which the oil has been added.

2. Chop the leeks, break the cauliflower into florets.

3. Combine the soya 'meat' with the leeks, cauliflower, rice, peas, herbs and seasoning. Turn into a casserole and cover with boiling water (include the stock in which the soya 'meat' was soaked).

4. Cover and cook at 325°F/170°C (Gas Mark 3) for about 1 hour, or until all the ingredients are cooked. Stir in the quartered tomatoes just before serving.

Leek Pie

Imperial/Metric	American
4 oz (115g) butter	½ cupful butter
1 medium onion, sliced	1 medium onion, sliced
1 lb (455g) leeks, cleaned and sliced	1 pound leeks, cleaned and sliced
¼ pint (140ml) single cream	⅔ cupful light cream
1 tablespoonful wholemeal flour	1 tablespoonful wholewheat flour
Sea salt	Sea salt
Freshly ground black pepper	Freshly ground black pepper
1 lb (455g) wholemeal shortcrust pastry (see page 61)	1 pound wholewheat shortcrust pastry (see page 61)
1 egg, beaten (to glaze)	1 egg, beaten (to glaze)

1. Melt half the butter and fry the onion until transparent.

2. Add the leeks along with the rest of the butter and cook slowly for about 10 minutes.

3. Combine the cream and flour and stir this mixture into the vegetables.

4. Cook for a couple of minutes to thicken.

5. Season well with salt and pepper (or nutmeg, if you prefer).

6. Make a pie case with the pastry and fill with the leek mixture. Cover with pastry and seal well at the edges.

7. Glaze with beaten egg and make a hole in the centre to allow steam to escape.

8. Bake at 350°F/180°C (Gas Mark 4) for 45 minutes until the pastry begins to brown.

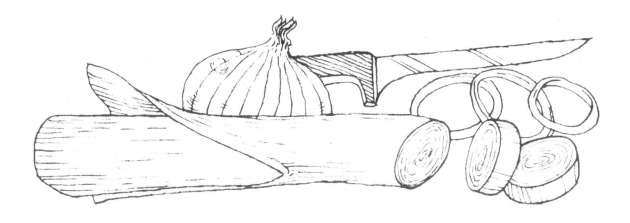

Stuffed Marrow

Serves 6

Imperial/Metric	American
1 medium marrow	1 medium summer squash
1 medium onion, finely chopped	1 medium onion, finely chopped
2 cloves garlic, finely chopped	2 cloves garlic, finely chopped
1 tablespoonful vegetable oil	1 tablespoonful vegetable oil
¾ lb (340g) cooked brown rice	2 cupsful cooked brown rice
¾ lb (340g) buckwheat groats	2 cupsful buckwheat groats
4 oz (115g) chopped hazelnuts	¾ cupful chopped hazelnuts
1 medium tin tomatoes	1 medium can tomatoes
1 tablespoonful marjoram	1 tablespoonful marjoram
1 teaspoonful sea salt	1 teaspoonful sea salt
1 teaspoonful freshly ground black pepper	1 teaspoonful freshly ground black pepper
½ pint (285ml) water	1¼ cupsful water
10 oz (285g) grated Cheddar cheese	2½ cupsful grated Cheddar cheese
Pinch of cayenne	Pinch of cayenne

1.   Cut the marrow (summer squash) in half lengthways and scoop out the seeds. Lay the halves side by side in an ovenproof dish lined with sufficient tin foil to wrap over the top before baking.

2.   Sauté the onion and garlic in the oil for 5 minutes.

3.   Stir in the rice and buckwheat, mixing them together well.

4.   Add all the other ingredients with the exception of the cheese and cayenne and cook for a few minutes.

5.   Spoon the mixture into the hollowed out sections of the marrow (summer squash). Sprinkle the top with grated cheese and cayenne.

6.   Bring the foil over the top and cook at 350°F/180°C (Gas Mark 4) for 1 hour or until the marrow (summer squash) is well cooked and soft.

Vegetables in Hollandaise Sauce

For sauce:

Imperial/Metric	American
2 tablespoonsful polyunsaturated margarine *or* butter	2 tablespoonsful polyunsaturated margarine *or* butter
3 tablespoonsful wholemeal flour	3 tablespoonsful wholewheat flour
¾ pint (425ml) water	2 cupsful water
Seasoning to taste	Seasoning to taste
1 tablespoonful milk *or* cream	1 tablespoonful milk *or* cream
1 egg yolk	1 egg yolk
1 tablespoonful lemon juice	1 tablespoonful lemon juice
Tarragon to taste	Tarragon to taste

For vegetable base:

Imperial/Metric	American
2 carrots	2 carrots
½ small cauliflower	½ small cauliflower
2 onions	2 onions
2 tablespoonsful peas (*or* your choice of mixed vegetables — broccoli and Brussels sprouts go well with this sauce)	2 tablespoonsful peas (*or* your choice of mixed vegetables — broccoli and Brussels sprouts go well with this sauce)

1. To make the sauce, heat one teaspoonful of the margarine, add it to the flour, stir and cook until brown.

2. Pour in the water gradually, stirring, and cook for a few minutes longer.

3. Dissolve the rest of the margarine in the hot water, add seasoning and remove the saucepan from the heat.

4. Mix together the milk and egg yolk. Add the lemon juice to the water, then the egg mixture, stirring slowly all the time so the egg does not curdle.

5. Sprinkle in a little tarragon and pour the sauce over the cooked, hot vegetables.

Note: The sauce also tastes delicious served at room temperature with a cold asparagus or green bean salad, or with battered, deep-fried mushrooms.

Bulgur Bake

Imperial/Metric	American
½ lb (225g) bulgur	1 cupful bulgur
1 oz (30g) margarine *or* butter	2½ tablespoonsful margarine *or* butter
1 large onion	1 large onion
1 large pepper	1 large pepper
1 pint (570ml) vegetable stock	2½ cupsful vegetable stock
Seasoning to taste	Seasoning to taste
2 eggs	2 eggs
Approx. ¼ pint (140ml) plain yogurt	⅔ cupful plain yogurt
2 oz (55g) grated Cheddar cheese	½ cupful grated Cheddar cheese
Good pinch of paprika	Good pinch of paprika

1.   Wash the bulgur, and drain well.

2.   Melt half the fat in a saucepan and gently sauté the sliced onion and pepper until they begin to soften, then set aside.

3.   Add the rest of the fat to the pan with the bulgur and cook for a few minutes to brown lightly. Pour in the stock, season to taste, bring to the boil and then cover and simmer for 15 minutes or until most of the stock has been absorbed. Drain off any excess liquid.

4.   Add the onion and pepper to the bulgur with the well-beaten eggs and enough yogurt to make the mixture creamy.

5.   Spoon into a greased ovenproof dish and sprinkle with the grated cheese and paprika. Bake at 350°F/180°C (Gas Mark 4) for 20-30 minutes, or until set.

Dieting the Wholefood Way

Piperade

Imperial/Metric	American
2 oz (55g) polyunsaturated margarine	¼ cupful polyunsaturated margarine
2 small green peppers	2 small green peppers
2 small onions	2 small onions
4 large tomatoes	4 large tomatoes
8 eggs	8 eggs
Seasoning to taste	Seasoning to taste
Herbs	Herbs

1. Melt the margarine and lightly fry the chopped pepper and onion. Add the sliced tomatoes and cook for 1 minute longer.

2. Beat the eggs, add seasoning and herbs, then add to the pan in which the vegetables are cooking. Stir, whilst cooking gently, until the eggs are set. Serve at once.

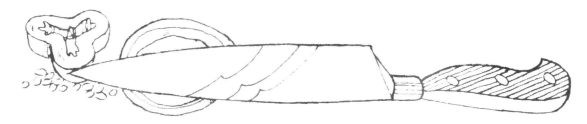

Baked Courgettes

Imperial/Metric	American
2 lb (900g) courgettes, sliced	2 pounds zucchini, sliced
1 medium onion, thinly sliced	1 medium onion, thinly sliced
14 oz (395g) tin tomatoes	1 medium can tomatoes
6 tablespoonsful olive oil	½ cupful olive oil
6 tablespoonsful vegetable stock	½ cupful vegetable stock
1 teaspoonful raw cane sugar	1 teaspoonful raw cane sugar
2 cloves garlic, crushed	2 cloves garlic, crushed
2 tablespoonsful parsley, finely chopped	2 tablespoonsful parsley, finely chopped
Seasoning	Seasoning
2 tablespoonsful wholemeal breadcrumbs	2 tablespoonsful wholewheat breadcrumbs
2 oz (55g) large, black olives	2 ounces large, black olives

1.   Grease a casserole dish and put a layer of courgettes (zucchini) in the bottom.

2.   Put in a layer of sliced onion followed by tomatoes and continue in this way until all the vegetables are used up.

3.   Mix together 4 tablespoonsful of olive oil, stock, sugar, garlic and parsley and season well with sea salt and freshly ground black pepper. Pour this mixture over the vegetables.

4.   Sprinkle with breadcrumbs, pour over the rest of the oil, and bake in a moderate oven at 350°F/180°C (Gas Mark 4) for 1 hour.

5.   Garnish with black olives.

Note: Sliced new potatoes, aubergines (eggplants) and peppers can also be used to make up the layers in this dish.

Illustrated opposite page 128.

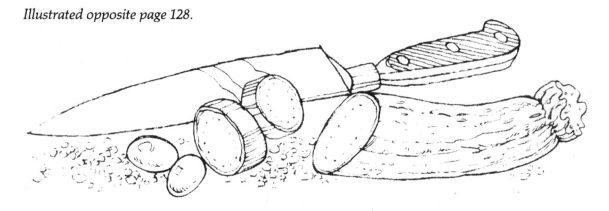

Beansprout Casserole

Imperial/Metric	American
1 large onion	1 large onion
4 sticks celery	4 stalks celery
2 oz (55g) polyunsaturated margarine *or* butter	¼ cupful polyunsaturated margarine *or* butter
⅓ pint (200ml) vegetable stock	¾ cupful vegetable stock
6 oz (170g) beansprouts	3 cupsful beansprouts
4 oz (115g) cooked peas	¾ cupful cooked peas
3 oz (85g) walnut pieces	⅔ cupful English walnut pieces
Seasoning	Seasoning
Soya sauce	Soy sauce
2 oz (55g) wholemeal breadcrumbs	1 cupful wholewheat breadcrumbs
Watercress to garnish	Watercress to garnish

1.   Chop the onion and celery into small pieces. Melt the fat in a frying pan (skillet) and sauté the onion and celery for 5 minutes, stirring frequently.

2.   Add the vegetable stock, bring to the boil and cook for just a few minutes.

3.   Mix the prepared vegetables with the beansprouts, cooked peas and walnut pieces, and transfer to an ovenproof dish. Season to taste and add soya sauce. Top with breadcrumbs.

4.   Bake at 350°F/180°C (Gas Mark 4) for about 20 minutes, or until the ingredients are cooked. Serve at once, decorated with sprigs of watercress.

Green Beans with Yogurt

Imperial/Metric	American
1½ lb (680g) French beans	1½ pounds snap beans
Parsley	Parsley
Dill	Dill
1 spring onion	1 scallion
1 teaspoonful fennel seeds	1 teaspoonful fennel seeds
Seasoning to taste	Seasoning to taste
¼ pint (140ml) plain yogurt	⅔ cupful plain yogurt
Soya 'bacon' bits (optional)	Soy *'Baco-Bits'* (optional)

1.   Top and tail the beans, and steam or boil them for about 10 minutes, or until cooked but still crisp. Drain then rinse with cold water, and put into a bowl.

2.   Chop the parsley, dill and onion coarsely, and mix with the beans together with the fennel seed and seasoning. If possible, let the mixture stand for a short while for the flavours to mingle, but not necessarily in a refrigerator.

3.   Serve topped with the yogurt, which can be mixed into the other ingredients at the table. Soya 'bacon' bits make a crisp, salty contrast to the delicately flavoured beans and yogurt.

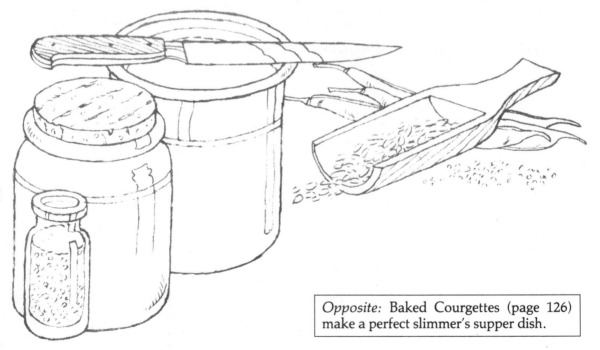

Opposite: Baked Courgettes (page 126) make a perfect slimmer's supper dish.

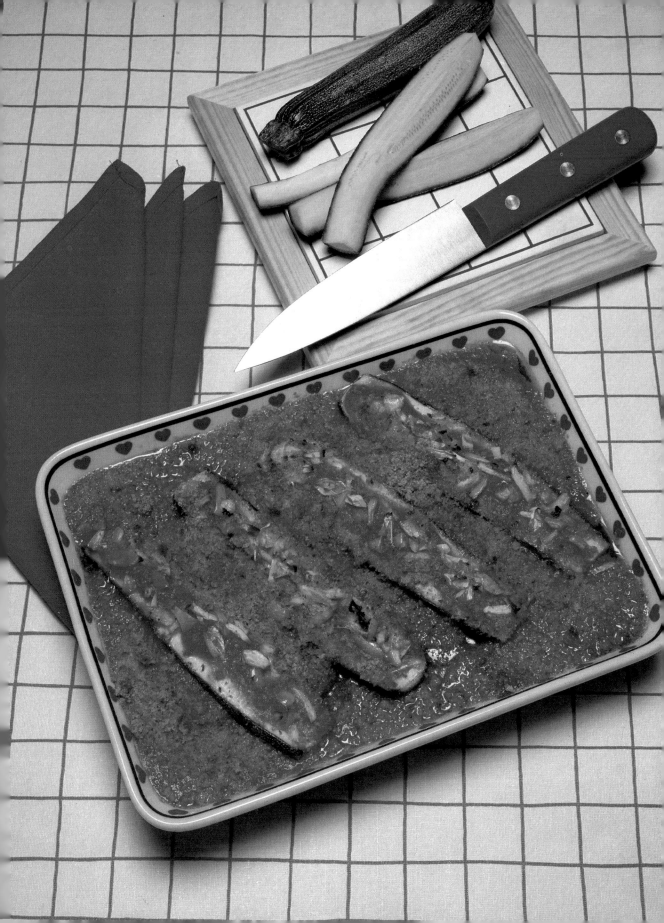

Mushroom Cabbage Rolls

Imperial/Metric	American
8 large Chinese cabbage leaves	8 large Chinese cabbage leaves
3 tablespoonsful vegetable oil	3 tablespoonsful vegetable oil
1 large onion	1 large onion
1 clove garlic, crushed	1 clove garlic, crushed
6 oz (170g) mushrooms	3 cupsful mushrooms
4 oz (115g) sunflower seeds	1 cupful sunflower seeds
Approx. 10 oz (285g) mixed cooked grains*	Approx. 1⅔ cupsful mixed cooked grains*
Seasoning to taste	Seasoning to taste
Tomato sauce to serve (optional)	Tomato sauce to serve (optional)

1.   Trim the stalks of the cabbage leaves, then drop the leaves into boiling salted water and cook for 2 minutes. Drain well and set aside to cool.

2.   Heat the oil in a saucepan and gently sauté the sliced onion and crushed garlic until the onion begins to go transparent. Add the sliced mushrooms and cook a few minutes more, stirring frequently.

3.   Stir in the sunflower seeds and cooked grain, then season well.

4.   Place an equal amount of the filling near the base of each of the leaves, and roll them up carefully to form a parcel, turning the sides in so that the filling is held in place.

5.   Arrange side by side in a shallow ovenproof dish, cover, and bake at 350°F/180°C (Gas Mark 4) for about 30 minutes, or until cooked. Serve hot. A spicy tomato sauce goes well.

* Any mixture of cooked grains can be used, so this is an ideal recipe for making use of leftovers. Or use one grain only, if you prefer.

Opposite: Winter salads to keep the slimmer happy. Red Cabbage and Walnut Salad (page 139) and Nutty Mushroom Salad (page 138).

Marrow Rings with Millet Stuffing

Imperial/Metric	American
4 thick marrow slices	4 thick summer squash slices
2 tablespoonsful vegetable oil	2 tablespoonsful vegetable oil
1 small onion, finely chopped	1 small onion, finely chopped
4 oz (115g) cooked millet	½ cupful cooked millet
4 oz (115g) cashew nut pieces	¾ cupful cashew nut pieces
2 tablespoonsful chopped parsley	2 tablespoonsful chopped parsley
1-2 teaspoonsful marjoram	1-2 teaspoonsful marjoram
Seasoning to taste	Seasoning to taste
Cheese or white sauce to serve	Cheese or white sauce to serve

1.   Peel the marrow (summer squash) slices, scoop out the seeds, and stand the rings in a shallow greased ovenproof dish or tin.

2.   In a saucepan, heat the oil and gently fry the finely chopped onion for just a few minutes to soften.

3.   Stir in the millet, cashew nuts, parsley, marjoram and seasoning. Divide the mixture between the marrow rings, packing it in tightly.

4.   Cover the dish. (If it doesn't have a lid, use silver foil, tucking it over the edges so that the ingredients cook in their own steam.)

5.   Bake at 350°F/180°C (Gas Mark 4) for 30-45 minutes or until the marrow is tender. Serve hot with cheese or white sauce.

Endive Omelette

Imperial/Metric	American
1 medium endive	1 medium chicory
3 tablespoonsful vegetable oil	3 tablespoonsful vegetable oil
6 eggs	6 eggs
Seasoning to taste	Seasoning to taste
Chives to garnish	Chives to garnish

1.   Trim the tough base of the stem, remove any wilted or damaged leaves, and wash the endive before shredding it coarsely. Steam for 5 minutes, then drain well and squeeze to make sure it is as dry as possible.

2.   Heat the oil in a large frying pan (skillet) and cook the endive (chicory) for a few minutes more, stirring frequently.

3.   Beat the eggs with the seasoning and pour them over the endive (chicory), tipping the pan so that the mixture spreads evenly.

4.   Continue cooking gently until the mixture begins to set, then flip the omelette over and cook the other side a few minutes more. (This is easiest to do if you hold a plate over the top of the pan, tip it so that the omelette rests on the plate and then slide it back into the pan.)

5.   Serve piping hot, garnished with the chives, then cut into individual wedges.

Aubergine Layers

Imperial/Metric	American
2 medium aubergines	2 medium eggplants
½ lb (225g) tomatoes	8 ounces tomatoes
4 oz (115g) Cheddar cheese	1 cupful Cheddar cheese
2 oz (55g) flaked *or* chopped blanched almonds	½ cupful slivered *or* chopped blanched almonds
2 teaspoonsful thyme	2 teaspoonsful thyme
Seasoning to taste	Seasoning to taste

1.   Cook the aubergines (eggplants) in boiling water until tender. Drain, cut off the top and tail, and slice evenly.

2.   Slice the tomatoes and grate the cheese.

3.   Place a layer of aubergine (eggplant) in a casserole, cover with half the tomatoes, some nuts, cheese and a sprinkling of herbs and seasoning.

4.   Repeat, finishing with cheese and herbs on top.

5.   Bake for 10 minutes at 400°F/200°C (Gas Mark 6).

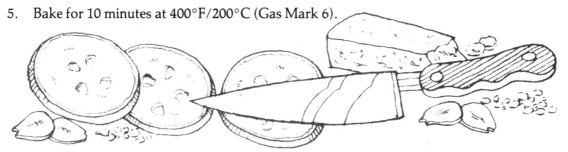

Ratatouille

Imperial/Metric	American
4 tomatoes	4 tomatoes
2 large onions	2 large onions
1 lb (455g) marrow *or* courgettes (*or* 1 cucumber)	1 pound summer squash *or* zucchini (*or* 1 cucumber)
2 large aubergines	2 large eggplants
1 small green pepper	1 small green pepper
6 tablespoonsful vegetable oil	6 tablespoonsful vegetable oil
Seasoning to taste	Seasoning to taste
1 clove of garlic, crushed (*or* garlic salt)	1 clove of garlic, crushed (*or* garlic salt)
1 small tin sweetcorn	1 small can sweetcorn
Grated cheese (optional)	Grated cheese (optional)

1.   Skin and slice the tomatoes, onions, marrow (or courgettes or cucumber).

2.   Chop the aubergines (eggplants) and green pepper, heat the oil and add all the prepared vegetables, seasoning and garlic.

3.   Stir well, cover the saucepan and simmer for 30-45 minutes. (If the oven is alight you can cook your ratatouille on the bottom shelf — keep it covered and make sure the vegetables have plenty of liquid to cook in.)

4.   When almost cooked, open the tin of sweetcorn, drain it and stir it into the ratatouille. Return to the heat briefly.

5.   Top with grated cheese and put it under the grill to melt the cheese.

Illustrated opposite page 97.

Fennel and Carrot Soufflé

Imperial/Metric	American
½ lb (225g) carrots	8 ounces carrots
4 fennel bulbs	4 fennel bulbs
Seasoning to taste	Seasoning to taste
2 oz (55g) grated Parmesan cheese	½ cupful grated Parmesan cheese
3 egg yolks	3 egg yolks
5 egg whites	5 egg whites

1. Slice the peeled carrots and boil or steam them until soft.

2. Trim, wash, and — in a separate pan — cook the fennel bulbs gently in boiling water for about 30 minutes, or until tender.

3. Drain both the vegetables and purée them in a blender. Mix well, and set aside to cool slightly.

4. When ready, add seasoning and grated cheese to the vegetable purée, then beat in the egg yolks.

5. Whisk the egg whites until stiff, and fold them into the first mixture.

6. Spoon into a greased medium-sized soufflé dish and bake at 375°F/190°C (Gas Mark 5) for 25-30 minutes, or until the soufflé is puffed up and lightly browned. Serve immediately.

Stewed Artichoke Hearts

Serves 6

Imperial/Metric	American
2 medium onions, finely chopped	2 medium onions, finely chopped
¼ pint (140ml) olive oil	⅔ cupful olive oil
1 tablespoonful wholemeal flour	1 tablespoonful wholewheat flour
Juice of 2 lemons	Juice of 2 lemons
4 oz (115g) shallots	4 ounces shallots
1 lb (455g) small, round, new potatoes	1 pound small, round, new potatoes
2 × 14 oz (395g) tins artichoke hearts	2 medium cans artichoke hearts
1 teaspoonful dill	1 teaspoonful dill
Seasoning	Seasoning

1. In a wide, shallow pan (a wok would be suitable) fry the onion in the oil until transparent.

2. Add the flour slowly and stir until you have a smooth, thin roux.

3. Add the lemon juice, shallots and scrubbed new potatoes.

4. Simmer gently for 30 minutes or so until the potatoes are becoming tender. Some water may be added to cover the potatoes.

5. Drain the artichoke hearts and add them to the pan with the dill. Baste well and simmer for a further 15 minutes. The liquid should have mostly evaporated leaving a delicious, thick, lemony sauce.

Slimmers' Pancakes

For batter:

Imperial/Metric	American
4 oz (115g) plain wholemeal flour	1 cupful plain wholewheat flour
Pinch of sea salt	Pinch of sea salt
1 egg	1 egg
½ pint (285ml) milk, *or* half milk and half water	1⅓ cupful milk, *or* half milk and half water

For filling:

Imperial/Metric	American
½ lb (225g) cottage cheese	1 cupful cottage cheese
1 small cucumber	1 small cucumber
Chopped chives	Chopped chives
Seasoning to taste	Seasoning to taste
⅓ pint (200ml) tomato juice	¾ cupful tomato juice

1. Sieve together the flour and salt, then add the egg and stir briefly.

2. Gradually pour in the liquid, stirring continually to blend in the flour and remove lumps, and continue beating until you have a smooth creamy batter. Leave in the fridge for at least 30 minutes, then beat again before using.

3. Cook pancakes and leave in a warm place.

4. Mix together the cottage cheese, chopped cucumber, most of the chives, and seasoning. Fill the pancakes with the cheese mixture, and fold.

5. Heat the tomato juice gently and spread a little over each pancake, then sprinkle with the rest of the chopped chives. Serve at once.

Slimmers' Spaghetti

Imperial/Metric	American
½ lb (225g) wholemeal spaghetti	8 ounces wholewheat spaghetti
4 tablespoonsful vegetable oil	⅓ cupful vegetable oil
2 large onions, chopped	2 large onions, chopped
6 oz (170g) mushrooms, chopped	3 cupsful mushrooms, chopped
4 tomatoes, chopped	4 tomatoes, chopped
Seasoning to taste	Seasoning to taste
Parmesan cheese (optional)	Parmesan cheese (optional)

1. Heat a large pan of water and add the spaghetti; cook for about 10 minutes until soft.

2. Meanwhile, heat the oil in a separate pan and then add the chopped vegetables. (If the mixture is too dry you may need to add a little extra water.)

3. Simmer for 5 minutes, season generously, and serve over the well-drained spaghetti.

4. Sprinkle with Parmesan cheese if liked.

Tofu Burgers

Imperial/Metric	American
2 lb (900g) tofu	4 cupsful tofu
4½ tablespoonsful grated carrot	4½ tablespoonsful grated carrot
1 small onion *or* several spring onions, finely chopped	1 small onion *or* several scallions, finely chopped
2 tablespoonsful sunflower seeds	2 tablespoonsful sunflower seeds
1 teaspoonful sea salt	1 teaspoonful sea salt
2 tablespoonsful raisins	2 tablespoonsful raisins
Vegetable oil for deep-frying	Vegetable oil for deep-frying

1. Drain the tofu between two layers of clean tea-towels and press it down with a weight for about 30 minutes.

2. Place the tofu in a bowl and knead it for a few minutes.

3. Add the remaining ingredients and knead them together for a few minutes until well mixed.

4. Shape the mixture into burgers and deep-fry them for a few minutes until done.

Asparagus Quiche with Yogurt

For base:

Imperial/Metric	American
4 oz (115g) wholemeal breadcrumbs	2 cupsful wholewheat breadcrumbs
Small carton plain yogurt	Small carton plain yogurt
Seasoning to taste	Seasoning to taste

For filling:

Imperial/Metric	American
½ lb (225g) fresh *or* frozen asparagus tips	8 ounces fresh *or* frozen asparagus tips
3 eggs	3 eggs
¼ pint (140ml) milk	⅔ cupful milk
Small carton plain yogurt	Small carton plain yogurt
Seasoning to taste	Seasoning to taste
Fresh parsley	Fresh parsley
4 oz (115g) Gruyère *or* Cheddar cheese	1 cupful Gruyère *or* Cheddar cheese

1. Combine the breadcrumbs with the yogurt and seasoning, tip into an 8 in. (20cm) flan dish, and press the mixture down to form an even lining on the base and sides.

2. Lightly steam the asparagus if fresh; cook according to instructions if frozen. Drain well.

3. Beat the eggs, add the milk, yogurt, seasoning and parsley.

4. Arrange most of the asparagus in the flan case, keeping a few pieces for decoration.

5. Spread the grated cheese over the asparagus, then pour in the egg mixture and top with the reserved asparagus tips.

6. Bake at 375°F/190°C (Gas Mark 5) for 30-35 minutes, or until set. Serve hot or warm.

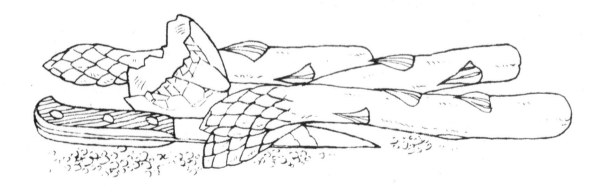

Spring Risotto

Imperial/Metric	American
4 tablespoonsful olive oil	4 tablespoonsful olive oil
1 onion, chopped	1 onion, chopped
1¼ lb (565g) long-grain brown rice	2½ cupsful long-grain brown rice
1½ pints (850ml) boiling water	4 cupsful boiling water
1 small cauliflower	1 small cauliflower
1 lb (455g) broccoli (heads only)	1 pound broccoli (heads only)
2 leeks, chopped	2 leeks, chopped
Sea salt, freshly ground black pepper and cayenne pepper	Sea salt, freshly ground black pepper and cayenne pepper
½ lb (225g) spinach, chopped	8 ounces spinach, chopped
4 oz (115g) strong Cheddar cheese, grated	1 cupful strong Cheddar cheese, grated
4 spring onions, finely chopped	4 scallions, finely chopped

1. Heat half the oil in a heavy saucepan and sauté the onion for 5 minutes.

2. Add the rice, stirring well to coat all the grains in oil, then add the boiling water and a pinch of sea salt. Cover and simmer for 40 minutes.

3. Heat the remaining oil in a heavy casserole. Sauté the cauliflower florets, broccoli, leeks and seasonings together, stirring gently for about 10 minutes.

4. Add the spinach, stirring for a few minutes whilst it reduces in size.

5. Add the cooked rice and half the cheese, sprinkle the remaining cheese and cayenne on top and grill until the cheese is melted and golden.

6. Sprinkle with the spring onions (scallions) and serve.

Nutty Mushroom Salad

Imperial/Metric	American
6 oz (170g) mushrooms	3 cupsful mushrooms
2 oz (55g) walnut pieces	½ cupful English walnut pieces
½ teaspoonful sea salt	½ teaspoonful sea salt
3 tablespoonsful sunflower oil	3 tablespoonsful sunflower oil
2 tablespoonsful lemon juice	2 tablespoonsful lemon juice
1 teaspoonful honey	1 teaspoonful honey
1 teaspoonful chopped fresh ginger *or*	1 teaspoonful chopped fresh ginger *or*
½ teaspoonful ground ginger	½ teaspoonful ground ginger
Small bunch washed watercress	Small bunch washed watercress

1. Wash, dry and thinly slice the mushrooms, then place them in a salad bowl with the walnuts.

2. Shake the salt, oil, lemon juice, honey and ginger together in a jar until thoroughly blended.

3. Pour the dressing over the mushrooms and walnuts and pile the mixture into the centre of the bowl.

4. Garnish the edges with watercress.

Illustrated opposite page 129.

Strawberry and Cucumber Salad

Imperial/Metric	American
1 small cucumber	1 small cucumber
12 large strawberries	12 large strawberries
2 tablespoonsful white wine vinegar	2 tablespoonsful white wine vinegar
Seasoning to taste	Seasoning to taste

1. Peel the cucumber and slice it finely.

2. Wash and hull the strawberries, drain them well and cut them into even slices.

3. Arrange the slices on a serving plate, first an outer circle of cucumber slices, then a slightly overlapping circle of strawberries, and so on, finishing with a central circle of strawberry slices.

4. Sprinkle with white wine vinegar, season lightly and chill well before serving.

Red Cabbage and Walnut Salad

Imperial/Metric	American
½ small red cabbage	½ small red cabbage
10-12 green grapes	10-12 green grapes
1 oz (30g) broken walnuts	¼ cupful broken English walnuts
Vinaigrette dressing (page 81)	Vinaigrette dressing (page 81)

1. Clean and shred the cabbage.

2. Mix it with the whole or halved grapes, and the nuts.

3. Add Vinaigrette dressing just before serving.

Illustrated opposite page 129.

Greek Summer Salad

Imperial/Metric	American
1 lettuce	1 lettuce
12 spring onions	12 scallions
6 large, firm tomatoes	6 large, firm tomatoes
½ cucumber, scored with a fork	½ cucumber, scored with a fork
12 sprigs of fresh mint, chopped	12 sprigs of fresh mint, chopped
1 teaspoonful dried marjoram *or* oregano	1 teaspoonful dried marjoram *or* oregano
4 tablespoonsful olive oil	4 tablespoonsful olive oil
2 tablespoonsful lemon juice	2 tablespoonsful lemon juice
Seasoning to taste	Seasoning to taste
6 oz (170g) Féta cheese	¾ cupful Féta cheese
18 black olives	18 black olives

1. Wash the lettuce, then drain it and divide it into leaves. Roll up each leaf and slice it finely.

2. Scatter the lettuce on a large serving dish.

3. Chop the spring onions (scallions), then slice tomatoes and cucumber and arrange them on the lettuce. Garnish with the onions and herbs.

4. Beat together the oil, lemon juice and seasoning and pour the dressing over the salad.

5. Crumble the cheese over the top of the salad and garnish with black olives.

Illustrated opposite page 81.

Beetroot and Egg Salad

Imperial/Metric	American
1 lb (455g) cooked beetroot	1 pound cooked beet
1 onion	1 onion
4 hard-boiled eggs	4 hard-boiled eggs
Approx. ¼ pint (140ml) Vinaigrette dressing (page 81)	Approx. ⅔ cupful Vinaigrette dressing (page 81)
Chopped fresh parsley	Chopped fresh parsley

1. Peel and grate the beetroot and the onion.

2. Cut the eggs in half and remove the yolks. Rub the yolks through a fine sieve and chop the whites into small pieces.

3. Put the beetroot, onion, egg yolks and dressing into a bowl and mix them gently.

4. Garnish the salad with chopped egg white and parsley.

Lentil Salad

Imperial/Metric	American
½ lb (225g) brown lentils	1 cupful brown lentils
4 tablespoonsful Vinaigrette dressing (page 81)	4 tablespoonsful Vinaigrette dressing (page 81)
1 small red pepper	1 small red pepper
1 onion	1 onion
2 sticks of celery	2 stalks of celery
Sea salt and freshly ground black pepper	Sea salt and freshly ground black pepper
Chopped parsley	Chopped parsley

1. Cover the lentils with boiling water and leave them to soak for 30 minutes. Drain, cover with fresh water, bring to the boil and cook gently until tender (about 40 minutes). Drain well and mix with the French dressing while still warm.

2. Core, de-seed and chop the pepper. Peel and slice the onion and chop the celery. Add all these ingredients to the lentil mixture. Season well and chill.

3. Garnish with chopped parsley before serving.

Beansprout and Apple Salad with Coconut Dressing

Imperial/Metric	*American*
1 small green cabbage	1 small green cabbage
1 large apple	1 large apple
1 cupful beansprouts (alfalfa *or* mung)	1¼ cupsful beansprouts (alfalfa *or* mung)
4 tablespoonsful cider vinegar	4 tablespoonsful cider vinegar
Pinch of raw cane sugar	Pinch of raw cane sugar
4 tablespoonsful natural yogurt	4 tablespoonsful natural yogurt
1 oz (30g) unsweetened, desiccated coconut	⅓ cupful unsweetened, desiccated coconut
Pinch of sea salt	Pinch of sea salt
Toasted, unsweetened, desiccated coconut to garnish	Toasted, unsweetened, desiccated coconut to garnish

1. Shred the cabbage and apple finely and put them into a serving bowl with the beansprouts.

2. Make a dressing with the cider vinegar, sugar, yogurt, coconut and salt to taste.

3. Pour the dressing over the salad and mix it in well. Garnish with toasted desiccated coconut.

Prune, Walnut and Cottage Cheese Salad

Imperial/Metric	*American*
1 large lettuce	1 large lettuce
½ lb (225g) plain cottage cheese	1 cupful plain cottage cheese
3 oz (85g) chopped walnuts	⅔ cupful chopped English walnuts
½ lb (225g) prunes, soaked and stoned	1½ cupsful prunes, soaked and stoned
Vinaigrette dressing (optional) (page 81)	Vinaigrette dressing (optional) (page 81)

1. Arrange the lettuce on a serving dish.

2. Pile the cottage cheese in the centre and garnish with the walnuts.

3. Chop the prunes and sprinkle them around the edge of the dish. If used, serve the dressing separately.

Tofu Guacamole

Imperial/Metric	American
1 ripe avocado	1 ripe avocado
1½ lb (680g) tofu	3 cupsful tofu
3 tablespoonsful vegetable oil *or* mayonnaise	3 tablespoonsful vegetable oil *or* mayonnaise
2 teaspoonsful sea salt	2 teaspoonsful sea salt
2 tablespoonsful lemon juice	2 tablespoonsful lemon juice
1 onion, chopped	1 onion, chopped

1.   Blend all the ingredients, adjusting the flavourings to suit your own taste. Use this as a dip for raw vegetable pieces or potato crisps, or as a salad dressing.

Baked Goodies

Honey and Wheatgerm Flapjacks

Imperial/Metric	American
3 oz (85g) polyunsaturated margarine	⅓ cupful polyunsaturated margarine
3 oz (85g) honey	¼ cupful honey
5 oz (140g) oats	1¼ cupsful rolled oats
1 oz (30g) wheatgerm	¼ cupful wheatgerm
Pinch of sea salt	Pinch of sea salt

1. Melt the margarine and honey together gently in a saucepan.

2. Stir in the oats, wheatgerm and salt, making sure they are well blended.

3. Spread the mixture evenly in a greased and floured 7 in. (18cm) tin, and press down lightly.

4. Bake at 350°F/180°C (Gas Mark 4) for about 20 minutes, or until turning golden.

5. Mark into portions while still warm, and remove carefully when cool but not completely cold.

Illustrated opposite page 145.

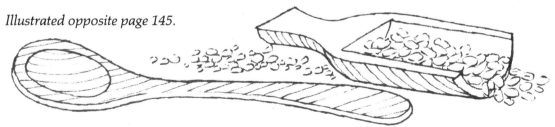

Pineapple Cake

Imperial/Metric	American
10 oz (285g) tofu	1¼ cupsful tofu
½ lb (225g) honey	1 cupful honey
4 tablespoonsful vegetable oil	¼ cupful vegetable oil
½ teaspoonful sea salt	½ teaspoonful sea salt
2 teaspoonsful baking powder	2 teaspoonsful baking powder
4 fl oz (120ml) soya milk	½ cupful soy milk
1 teaspoonful *or* a few drops pure vanilla essence (depending on type)	1 teaspoonful *or* a few drops pure vanilla essence (depending on type)
½ lb (225g) wholemeal flour	2 cupsful wholewheat flour
1 medium tin pineapple in its own juice	1 medium can pineapple in its own juice
2 tablespoonsful honey	2 tablespoonsful honey
1 tablespoonful arrowroot	1 tablespoonful arrowroot

1. Blend the tofu, honey, oil, salt, baking powder, soya milk and vanilla.

2. Add the flour and place the mixture in a greased cake tin.

3. Arrange circles of pineapple on top of the cake mixture.

4. Make the topping by mixing together the honey and a little pineapple juice and bringing it to the boil.

5. Add the arrowroot which has already been stirred into a little pineapple juice until dissolved thoroughly, and simmer until the liquid becomes clear.

6. Pour this sauce over the pineapple slices and bake the cake at 375°F/190°C (Gas Mark 5) for about 20 minutes.

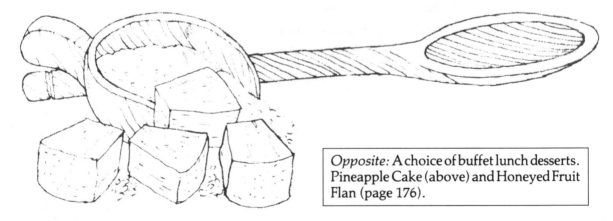

Opposite: A choice of buffet lunch desserts. Pineapple Cake (above) and Honeyed Fruit Flan (page 176).

Carob Cake

Imperial/Metric	American
½ lb (225g) honey	1 cupful honey
⅓ pint (200ml) vegetable oil	1 cupful vegetable oil
1 lb (455g) tofu	2 cupsful tofu
1 teaspoonful sea salt	1 teaspoonful sea salt
1 teaspoonful pure vanilla essence	1 teaspoonful pure vanilla essence
10 oz (285g) wholemeal flour	2½ cupsful wholewheat flour
6 oz (170g) carob powder	1½ cupsful carob powder

1. Blend the honey, oil, tofu, salt and vanilla essence.

2. Add the flour and carob and mix them well with a mixer or by hand.

3. Bake in a greased tin at 350°F/180°C (Gas Mark 4) for about 30 minutes.

Peanut Butter Bars

Imperial/Metric	American
½ lb (225g) wholemeal digestive biscuits	8 ounces Graham crackers
2 oz (55g) polyunsaturated margarine	¼ cupful polyunsaturated margarine
4 oz (115g) crunchy peanut butter	1 cupful crunchy peanut butter

1. Crush the digestive biscuits.

2. Mix with the melted margarine.

3. Whilst still warm, stir in the peanut butter and make sure all ingredients are thoroughly blended.

4. Turn into a lightly greased shallow tin and press down; chill.

5. When set, cut into even-sized bars.

Opposite: A wholefood biscuit barrel, with Honey and Wheatgerm Flapjacks (page 143), Macaroons (page 148) and Peanut Butter Bars (above).

Fruit and Nut Turnovers

For pastry:

Imperial/Metric	American
½ lb (225g) plain wholemeal flour	2 cupsful plain wholewheat flour
Pinch of sea salt	Pinch of sea salt
4 oz (115g) polyunsaturated margarine *or* butter	½ cupful polyunsaturated margarine *or* butter
3 oz (85g) raw cane sugar, powdered in grinder	½ cupful raw cane sugar, powdered in grinder
2 egg yolks	2 egg yolks

For filling:

Imperial/Metric	American
6 oz (170g) dried figs	1¼ cupsful dried figs
4 oz (115g) raisins	¾ cupful raisins
3 oz (85g) roasted almonds	¾ cupful roasted almonds
3 oz (85g) walnuts	¾ cupful English walnuts
2 tablespoonsful grated orange peel	2 tablespoonsful grated orange peel
Pinch of ground cloves	Pinch of ground cloves
1 teaspoonful mixed spice	1 teaspoonful mixed spice
Approx. 4 tablespoonsful clear honey	Approx. ⅓ cupful clear honey
1 egg white	1 egg white

1.   Sift together the flour and salt, then use fingertips to rub in the margarine to form a mixture like fine breadcrumbs. Stir in the sugar, then the egg yolks so you have a soft dough, and knead briefly. Cover the dough and chill.

2.   Wash the dried fruit then plump up in hot water. Drain, pat dry, and chop into small pieces. Either grind or chop the nuts as fine as possible. In a bowl mix together the fruit, nuts, peel, spices, and add enough honey to moisten the mixture.

3.   Roll out the dough and cut into small circles with a cutter or cup.

4.   Divide the fruit and nut mixture between the circles, putting it on one half only. Dampen the edges of the dough with a little of the egg white, fold to form a half-moon, and press the edges to seal.

5.   Brush the tops with more egg white, and prick or cut them to let air escape. Arrange on a lightly greased baking sheet.

6.   Cook the turnovers in a medium oven, 350°F/180°C (Gas Mark 4) for 20-30 minutes, or until the pastry is done. Delicious served hot, warm, or cold.

Gingerbread

Imperial/Metric	American
½ lb (225g) plain wholemeal flour	2 cupsful plain wholewheat flour
1 teaspoonful bicarbonate of soda	1 teaspoonful baking soda
2 teaspoonsful ground ginger	2 teaspoonsful ground ginger
4 oz (115g) raw cane sugar	⅔ cupful raw cane sugar
4 oz (115g) polyunsaturated margarine	½ cupful polyunsaturated margarine
1 tablespoonful molasses	1 tablespoonful molasses
1 egg	1 egg
Milk to mix	Milk to mix

1.   Sieve the dry ingredients into a bowl.

2.   Place the margarine and molasses in a saucepan and heat them gently until melted.

3.   Stir this mixture into the dry ingredients and beat in the egg and as much milk as necessary to make a thick batter.

4.   Line a 7 in. (18cm) square tin with greased greaseproof paper, and pour in the cake mixture.

5.   Bake the cake in the centre of the oven for 15 minutes at 350°F/180°C (Gas Mark 4), then for a further 45 minutes at 325°F/170°C (Gas Mark 3). Test that the cake is cooked before removing it from the oven, then let it cool for 10 minutes before placing it on an airing tray.

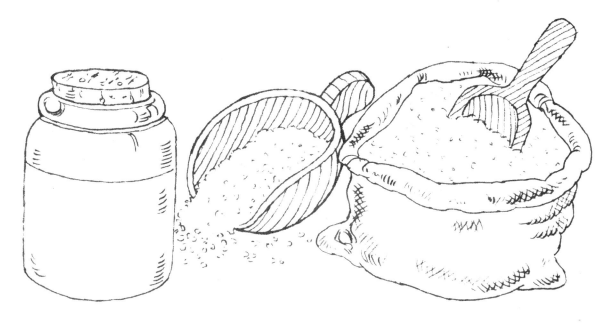

Marmalade Cake

Imperial/Metric	American
2 teaspoonsful baking powder	2 teaspoonsful baking powder
½ lb (225g) plain wholemeal flour	2 cupsful plain wholewheat flour
6 oz (170g) polyunsaturated margarine	¾ cupful polyunsaturated margarine
4 oz (115g) raw cane sugar	⅔ cupful raw cane sugar
4 tablespoonsful pure orange *or* grapefruit juice	4 tablespoonsful pure orange *or* grapefruit juice
1 egg	1 egg
2-3 tablespoonsful raw sugar marmalade	2-3 tablespoonsful raw sugar marmalade
1 tablespoonful grated orange peel (optional)	1 tablespoonful grated orange peel (optional)

1.   Sieve the baking powder into the flour, then mix all the ingredients together, making sure they are well blended.

2.   Turn the mixture into a greased loaf tin and bake the cake for about 1 hour at 350°F/180°C (Gas Mark 4).

Macaroons

Imperial/Metric	American
4 oz (115g) blanched almonds	1 cupful blanched almonds
Pinch of sea salt	Pinch of sea salt
2 egg whites	2 egg whites
½ lb (225g) raw cane sugar, powdered in grinder	1⅓ cupsful raw cane sugar, powdered in grinder
Natural vanilla essence	Natural vanilla essence
½ teaspoonful finely grated lemon peel (optional)	½ teaspoonful finely grated lemon peel (optional)
Rice paper (optional)	Rice paper (optional)

1.   Grind the almonds as fine as possible, then set aside.

2.   Add the salt to the egg whites and beat until the mixture is frothy. Gradually add the sugar, still beating continually so that eventually the mixture is quite stiff.

3.   Carefully fold in the ground almonds, a few drops of vanilla extract, and the lemon peel.

4.   Arrange the rice paper in tins and drop the prepared mixture onto it in small mounds, leaving room for the macaroons to spread. Alternatively drop them onto greased, floured baking sheets.

5.   Bake at 350°F/180°C (Gas Mark 4) for 20 minutes, or until a light golden colour. Cool slightly, remove from the tins, and tear or cut around each one to remove the excess rice paper. Leave to get completely cold before storing in a tin.

Illustrated opposite page 145.

Grape Tarts

For pastry:

Imperial/Metric	American
½ lb (225g) plain wholemeal flour	2 cupsful plain wholewheat flour
4 oz (115g) polyunsaturated margarine *or* butter	½ cupful polyunsaturated margarine *or* butter
Cold water to mix	Cold water to mix

For filling:

Imperial/Metric	American
5 oz (140g) white grapes	5 ounces white grapes
5 oz (140g) black grapes	5 ounces black grapes
½ lb (225g) Ricotta *or* cream cheese	1 cupful Ricotta *or* cream cheese
1 tablespoonful liqueur (optional)	1 tablespoonful liqueur (optional)
2 oz (55g) raw cane sugar, powdered in grinder	⅓ cupful raw cane sugar, powdered in grinder

1.   Sift the flour into a bowl and use your fingertips to rub in the margarine. When the mixture is like fine breadcrumbs, add cold water, a few drops at a time, and knead until you have a smooth, pliable dough. Wrap in aluminium foil or cling film and set aside to chill for at least 30 minutes.

2.   Roll out the pastry and use a cutter or cup to make approximately 12 small circles. Arrange these in lightly greased tart tins, prick with a fork, and bake at 375°F/190°C (Gas Mark 5) for 10 minutes, or until the pastry is cooked. Set aside to cool before removing carefully from the tins.

3.   Wash and dry the grapes.

4.   Use a wooden spoon to mash the cheese together with the liqueur until it is soft and completely smooth. Mix in the sugar, then stir in most of the grapes.

5.   Pile a little of the mixture into each of the tart shells and use the leftover grapes as decoration. Serve as soon as possible after preparing them.

Banana Tea Cake

Imperial/Metric	American
2 oz (55g) polyunsaturated margarine	¼ cupful polyunsaturated margarine
4 oz (115g) raw cane sugar	⅔ cupful raw cane sugar
1 lb (455g) ripe bananas, mashed	1 pound ripe bananas, mashed
7 oz (200g) plain wholemeal flour	1¾ cupful plain wholewheat flour
¼ pint (140ml) warm water	⅔ cupful warm water
1 oz (30g) chopped peel (optional)	2½ tablespoonsful chopped peel (optional)
1 oz (30g) chopped walnuts (optional)	¼ cupful chopped English walnuts (optional)

1. Melt the margarine, add the sugar and then the mashed banana.

2. Stir in the flour and add enough water to make the mixture fairly stiff.

3. Add the peel and walnuts, distributing them as evenly as possible.

4. Bake the cake in a greased tin at 350°F/180°C (Gas Mark 4) for 45 minutes to 1 hour.

Treacle Tart

Imperial/Metric	American
Pastry to line an 8 in. (20cm) flan dish (see page 61)	Pastry to line an 8 inch flan dish (see page 61)
2 oz (55g) molasses	2 tablespoonsful molasses
1-2 teaspoonsful lemon juice	1-2 teaspoonsful lemon juice
4 oz (115g) soft wholemeal breadcrumbs	2 cupsful soft wholewheat breadcrumbs

1. Line the flan dish with the rolled out pastry, and bake it 'blind' for 15 minutes at 400°F/200°C (Gas Mark 6).

2. In a saucepan warm the molasses and lemon juice together, then stir in the breadcrumbs, making sure they are coated evenly.

3. Pour mixture into the flan case and continue baking at 350°F/180°C (Gas Mark 4) for 30 minutes more. Serve hot or cold.

Tiger Nut Fingers

Makes 12

Imperial/Metric	*American*
2 oz (55g) fresh yeast	¼ cupful fresh yeast
1 dessertspoonful clear honey	2 teaspoonsful clear honey
½ pint (285ml) warm water	1⅓ cupsful warm water
1 lb (455g) wholemeal flour	4 cupsful wholewheat flour
1 dessertspoonful sesame salt (gomasio)	2 teaspoonsful sesame salt (gomasio)
4 oz (115g) tiger nuts	¾ cupful tiger nuts
A little beaten egg	A little beaten egg

1. Cream the yeast and honey to a smooth paste. Add the water and stir it in well, then leave the mixture in a warm place to start bubbling.

2. Put the flour and sesame salt (gomasio) into a large mixing bowl and stir them together.

3. Grind the tiger nuts to a fine powder using a liquidizer or coffee grinder, and then mix it into the flour.

4. Add the frothy yeast mixture to the flour and mix it in to form a dough.

5. Turn the dough out onto a well-floured board and knead it for 10-15 minutes. Return the dough to the bowl, cover it with a cloth and leave to rise in a warm place until it has doubled in size.

6. Knock back the dough for another few minutes, then divide it into 12 equal pieces. Knead each piece into a 6 in. (15cm) long 'finger' roll.

7. Place the rolls on a flat baking tray, spacing evenly apart, and brush them with the beaten egg, then leave them to rise in a warm place until the fingers look puffy and have nearly doubled in size again.

8. Bake the rolls at 400°F/200°C (Gas Mark 6) for 10 minutes.

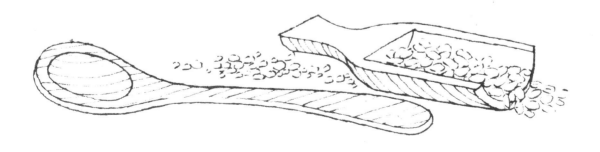

Fruit-Stuffed Plait

Makes 1 large plait

Imperial/Metric	American
2 oz (55g) fresh yeast	¼ cupful fresh yeast
1 dessertspoonful clear honey	2 teaspoonsful clear honey
½ pint (285ml) warm milk	1⅓ cupsful warm milk
1 lb 2 oz (500g) wholemeal flour	4½ cupsful wholewheat flour
1 teaspoonful sea salt	1 teaspoonful sea salt
1 beaten egg	1 beaten egg
A little extra beaten egg	A little extra beaten egg

Fruit filling:

Imperial/Metric	American
4 oz (115g) currants	⅔ cupful currants
2 oz (55g) sultanas	⅓ cupful golden seedless raisins
2 oz (55g) raisins	⅓ cupful raisins
2 oz (55g) mixed, cut peel	5 tablespoonsful mixed, cut peel
1 dessertspoonful clear honey	2 teaspoonsful clear honey

1.   Cream the yeast into the honey and add the warm milk. Leave the mixture in a warm place for the yeast to start bubbling.

2.   Place the flour and salt in a large mixing bowl and mix them together. Add the beaten egg to the frothy yeast mixture and then pour it into the flour, mixing well to form a dough.

3.   Turn the dough out onto a floured board and knead well for about 10 minutes, using plenty of extra flour. Return the dough to the bowl, cover it with a cloth and leave it to double in size in a warm place.

4.   While the dough is rising, make the fruit filling by mixing together the currants, sultanas (golden seedless raisins), raisins, cut peel and honey in a small bowl.

5.   Knock back the dough for a few minutes, then knead it into a rough rectangle shape. Roll the dough out quite thinly with a rolling pin, keeping the shape rectangular. Make ten slits in the dough, five on each side of the long side of the rectangle, (as in diagram A). Spoon the fruit filling carefully down the centre, and fold the side pieces of dough over the fruit (as shown in diagram B).

6.   Place the loaf on a flat baking tray and brush the surface of the loaf all over with the extra beaten egg, then leave to rise in a warm place.

7.   When the loaf looks adequately risen and puffed up, bake it at 400°F/200°C (Gas Mark 6)

for 10 minutes. Then reduce the heat to 350°F/180°C (Gas Mark 4) and continue to bake for a further 10 to 15 minutes.

A)

fruit filling

B)

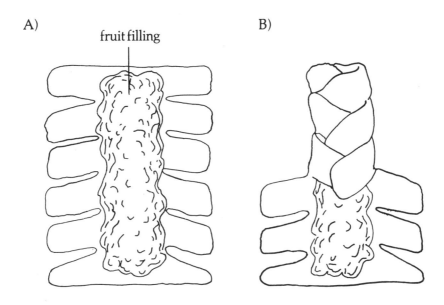

Cheese Scones

Imperial/Metric	American
½ lb (225g) self-raising wholemeal flour	2 cupsful self-raising wholewheat flour
Pinch each of sea salt and cayenne pepper	Pinch each of sea salt and cayenne pepper
1 oz (30g) polyunsaturated margarine	2½ tablespoonsful polyunsaturated margarine
2 oz (55g) Cheddar cheese, finely grated	½ cupful finely grated Cheddar cheese
Milk to mix	Milk to mix

1.   Sieve the flour and seasoning into a bowl.

2.   Rub in the margarine and cheese and enough milk to form a stiff dough.

3.   Turn the dough onto a floured board, knead it lightly, then roll it out to ½-¾ in. (1-1.5cm) thickness and cut it into rounds 2 in. (5cm) wide.

4.   Place the scones on a greased baking sheet and bake them at 425°F/220°C (Gas Mark 7) for about 15 minutes or until firm to touch.

Basic Wholemeal Bread

Makes 2 large loaves

Imperial/Metric	American
1 dessertspoonful honey	2 teaspoonsful honey
1½ oz (45g) fresh yeast	3½ tablespoonsful fresh yeast
1¼ pints (710ml) warm water	3¼ cupsful warm water
2½ lb (1¼ kilos) wholemeal flour	10 cupsful wholewheat flour
1 dessertspoonful sea salt	2 teaspoonsful sea salt
2 tablespoonsful vegetable oil	2 tablespoonsful vegetable oil

1.   Cream the honey and yeast together with a fork until they are well blended and there are no lumps of yeast left.

2.   Add ½ pint (¼ litre) of the warm water and mix well. Cover the container with a clean cloth and set it in a warm place for 10-15 minutes until the mixture starts to froth and bubble.

3.   Meanwhile, sieve the flour and salt into a large mixing bowl.

4.   When the yeast mixture is ready, beat the oil into it with a fork and pour it onto the flour. Add the remaining warm water and mix everything together until the dough is formed.

5.   Turn the dough out onto a well-floured board and knead it for about 10 minutes until it starts to feel smoother and more elastic, adding a little extra flour if necessary.

6.   Place the dough back into the mixing bowl and cover it with a clean cloth. Put it in a warm place for about 1 hour or so, or until it has doubled in bulk.

7.   Turn the dough out onto a floured board and knead it again for another few minutes, then divide the dough into two equal pieces and shape them into smooth loaves. Put them into well-oiled tins and set them in a warm place, covered with a cloth, to rise again.

8.   When the dough reaches the tops of the tins, place them in a hot oven at 400°F/200°C (Gas Mark 6) for 10 minutes, then turn down the heat to 350°F/180°C (Gas Mark 4) and continue to bake for a further 30-40 minutes.

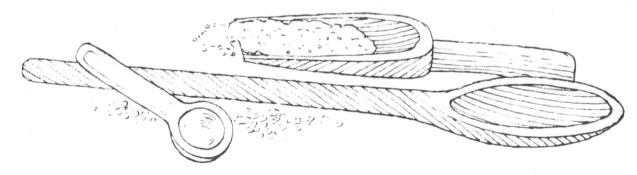

Quick, Unkneaded Wholemeal Bread

Makes 1 large loaf

Imperial/Metric	American
1 oz (30g) dried yeast	2½ tablespoonsful dried yeast
½ pint (285ml) warm water	1⅓ cupsful warm water
1 dessertspoonful honey	2 teaspoonsful honey
1 lb 6 oz (625g) wholemeal flour	5½ cupsful wholewheat flour
1 dessertspoonful sea salt	2 teaspoonsful sea salt

1.   Dissolve the dried yeast in the warm water, stirring it until it is all absorbed. Then add the honey and mix well. Set aside in the warmth for 10-15 minutes.

2.   Mix the flour and salt together, and set half of it aside in a separate bowl. Add the bubbly yeast mixture to one-half of the flour and mix it in well to form a thick batter. Whisk this by hand for about 10 minutes, or use an electric whisk for a couple of minutes.

3.   Add the rest of the flour and mix to form a smooth dough. Shape the dough into a smooth ball and put it into a well-oiled bread tin and leave to rise in a warm place for ½-¾ hour, until it reaches the top of the tin.

4.   Bake at 400°F/200°C (Gas Mark 6) for 10 minutes, then turn the heat down to 350°F/180°C (Gas Mark 4) and continue to bake for a further 30-40 minutes.

Sourdough Loaf

Makes 1 large loaf

Sourdough starter:

Imperial/Metric	American
1 dessertspoonful honey	2 teaspoonsful honey
1 oz (30g) fresh yeast	2½ tablespoonsful fresh yeast
½ pint (285ml) warm water	1⅓ cupsful warm water
6 oz (170g) wholemeal flour	1½ cupsful wholewheat flour

To add later:

Imperial/Metric	American
10 oz (285g) wholemeal flour	2½ cupsful wholewheat flour
1½ dessertspoonsful sea salt	3 teaspoonsful sea salt
1 dessertspoonful milk	2 teaspoonsful milk

1.   Cream the honey and the yeast together until no lumps are left, then add the warm water and stir well.

2.   Mix in the first quantity of flour and whisk it in to form a batter. Leave this mixture in a large mixing bowl covered with a plate, at room temperature from two to four days, depending on the strength of flavour required. You need to keep the batter in a large bowl to give it plenty of room to expand. Keep stirring it occasionally as the ingredients will separate and need to be reincorporated.

3.   When you consider the batter to be ready, stir in the remaining flour, salt and milk. Mix thoroughly to form a soft dough.

4.   Turn the dough out onto a floured surface and knead for about 10 minutes until it appears putty-like. Place it in a large mixing bowl and cover with a cloth. Leave in a warm place to rise.

5.   When it has just about doubled in bulk, turn the dough back out onto the floured surface and knead again for another few minutes. Have ready an oiled 2 lb (1 kg) loaf tin and press the dough into it. Leave to rise again somewhere warm until it fills the tin. Bake at 350°F/180°C (Gas Mark 4) for 45 minutes.

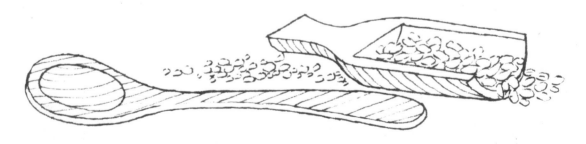

Sweet Potato Bloomer

Makes 1 large bloomer

Imperial/Metric	American
1 oz (30g) dried yeast	2½ tablespoonsful dried yeast
½ pint (285ml) warm water	1⅓ cupsful warm water
1 dessertspoonful clear honey	2 teaspoonsful clear honey
1 lb (455g) wholemeal flour	4 cupsful wholewheat flour
1 dessertspoonful sea salt	2 teaspoonsful sea salt
10 oz (285g) sweet potato *or* yam, peeled	10 ounces sweet potato *or* yam, peeled
A little beaten egg	A little beaten egg

1.   Put the yeast, warm water and honey into a small bowl, mix them well and leave the mixture in a warm place to start bubbling.

2.   Place the flour and salt in a large mixing bowl and mix them together.

3.   Chop the sweet potato into small pieces and boil it in water until soft and mushy, then mash it with a fork and add it to the flour, mixing well to avoid any lumps forming.

4.   Add the frothy yeast mixture and mix it in well to form a dough. Knead the dough well for 10-15 minutes until it is smooth and elastic, using extra flour if it seems too sticky. Return the dough to the bowl, cover it with a cloth and leave it in a warm place to double in size.

5.   Knock back the dough for another minute or so and then knead it into a smooth oblong shape. Place it on a flat baking tray, cover it with a cloth and leave it to rise in a warm place.

6.   When the loaf looks well risen, make four or five slanted slashes in the crust and brush it with the beaten egg.

7.   Bake at 400°F/200°C (Gas Mark 6) for 10 minutes, then reduce the heat to 350°F/180°C (Gas Mark 4) and continue to bake for a further 20-25 minutes.

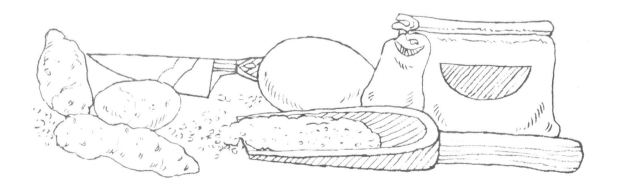

Rye Bread with Dill Seeds

Makes 1 large loaf

Imperial/Metric	American
1½ oz (45g) fresh yeast	3½ tablespoonsful fresh yeast
½ pint (285ml) warm water	1⅓ cupsful warm water
1 dessertspoonful honey	2 teaspoonsful honey
½ lb (225g) rye flour	2 cupsful rye flour
10 oz (285g) wholemeal flour	2½ cupsful wholewheat flour
1 dessertspoonful sea salt	2 teaspoonsful sea salt
½ oz (15g) dill seeds	1½ tablespoonsful dill seeds
A little milk	A little milk

1.   Dissolve the yeast in the warm water and stir in the honey. Leave the mixture in a warm place for 10-15 minutes until it starts to froth.

2.   Put the rye flour, wholemeal flour, salt and dill seeds into a large mixing bowl and stir them together. When the yeast mixture is ready, pour it into the centre of the flour and stir to form the dough. Roll the dough round with your hand until it is springy and kneadable, adding a little extra flour if the dough seems too sticky.

3.   Turn the dough out onto a floured board and knead for 10-15 minutes, by which time it should feel smoother and more pliable. Put the dough back into the mixing bowl and cover it with a clean cloth then leave it in a warm place until it has doubled in size.

4.   Knead again for another couple of minutes. Shape the dough carefully so that there are no cracks in the crust, and put it into a well-oiled 2 lb (1 kg) loaf tin. Let it rise again to the top of the tin.

5.   Brush the top of the crust with the extra milk and bake at 400°F/200°C (Gas Mark 6) for the first 10 minutes. Reduce the heat to 350°F/180°C (Gas Mark 4) and continue to bake the loaf for a further 30-40 minutes.

Yeasted Corn Bread

Makes 1 large loaf

Imperial/Metric	*American*
1½ oz (45g) fresh yeast	3½ tablespoonsful fresh yeast
1 dessertspoonful honey	2 teaspoonsful honey
½ pint (285ml) warm water	1⅓ cupful warm water
1 beaten egg	1 beaten egg
½ lb (225g) fine maize flour	2 cupsful fine cornmeal
14 oz (395g) wholemeal flour	3½ cupsful wholewheat flour
2 teaspoonsful sea salt	2 teaspoonsful sea salt
2 oz (55g) skimmed milk powder	⅔ cupful skimmed milk powder

1. Put the yeast, honey, warm water and beaten egg into a small mixing bowl and beat them well with a fork or whisk until they are all well blended. Set this mixture aside in the warmth so that the yeast can start to work.

2. Meanwhile put the maize flour (cornmeal), wholemeal flour, salt and dried milk into a large mixing bowl and stir them together. When the yeast mixture is good and frothy, pour it into the flour mixture and blend it in with a fork.

3. Roll the mixture around with your hands until it forms a proper dough, then turn it onto a floured board and knead it for about 15 minutes. Put it back in the bowl, set it aside in a warm place and let it double in bulk.

4. Knock back the dough for a few minutes and then carefully shape it for the tin. Place it in a well-greased 2 lb (1 kg) loaf tin and let it rise again until the top of the loaf just reaches the top of the tin. (It is important not to over-prove this type of bread, so don't let it rise any further.)

5. Bake at 400°F/200°C (Gas Mark 6) for 30 minutes, then turn down the heat to 350°F/180°C (Gas Mark 4) for a further 15 minutes. This bread is sweet, moist and yellowy and tends to be crumbly, so let it cool completely before slicing.

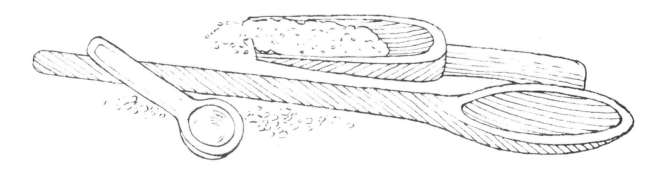

Wheatgerm Bread

Imperial/Metric	American
2½ lb (1¼ kilos) wholemeal flour	10 cupsful wholewheat flour
½ lb (225g) wheatgerm	2 cupsful wheatgerm
1 oz (30g) dried yeast	2½ cupsful dried yeast
1 teaspoonful honey *or* raw cane sugar	1 teaspoonful honey *or* raw cane sugar
1½ pints (850ml) warm water	3¾ cupsful warm water

1.   Combine the flour and wheatgerm in a warm bowl.

2.   Dissolve the yeast and honey (or sugar) in a third of the water, and leave in a draught-free spot until the mixture is frothy.

3.   Make a well in the flour, add the yeast mixture plus the rest of the water and, using your hands, mix well.

4.   Turn the dough onto a floured board and continue kneading until it is elastic. Leave covered in a warm place until the dough has doubled in size.

5.   Knead again for a few minutes, divide the dough into two, shape into two loaves and dust with flour.

6.   Place in two loaf tins, cover, and leave to rise again. Cook for 40-45 minutes at 375°F/190°C (Gas Mark 5).

Note: This is a highly nutritious bread, rather sweeter than usual, and very tasty in sandwiches. However, its high protein content makes it especially suitable as an accompaniment, lightly buttered, to salad.

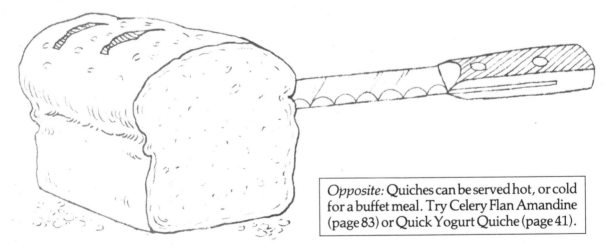

Opposite: Quiches can be served hot, or cold for a buffet meal. Try Celery Flan Amandine (page 83) or Quick Yogurt Quiche (page 41).

Caraway Cheese Bread

Imperial/Metric	*American*
½ lb (225g) wholemeal flour	2 cupsful wholewheat flour
3 tablespoonsful baking powder	3 tablespoonsful baking powder
Pinch of sea salt	Pinch of sea salt
6 oz (170g) polyunsaturated margarine	¾ cupful polyunsaturated margarine
1 large egg	1 large egg
6 oz (170g) Cheddar cheese, grated	1½ cupsful grated Cheddar cheese
1 oz (30g) caraway seeds	3½ tablespoonsful caraway seeds
¼ pint (140ml) milk	⅔ cupful milk

1. Sift together the flour, baking powder and salt.

2. Beat together the softened margarine, egg and cheese.

3. Stir in the seeds, then add the dry ingredients and mix thoroughly, stirring in the milk a drop at a time until the dough is firm but not too dry.

4. Grease a medium-sized tin and spoon the mixture into it evenly.

5. Bake at 350°F/180°C (Gas Mark 4) for 40-45 minutes, or until a knife comes out clean.

Opposite: Add variety to your meal with a selection of unusual breads such as Garlic and Sage Garland (page 162) and Black Peasant Bread (page 107).

Garlic and Sage Garland

Makes 1 garland — enough to serve 4 to 6

Imperial/Metric	American
1 oz (30g) fresh yeast	2½ tablespoonsful fresh yeast
1 teaspoonful honey	1 teaspoonful honey
¼ pint (140ml) warm water	⅔ cupful warm water
9 oz (255g) wholemeal flour	1¾ cupsful wholewheat flour
1 teaspoonful sea salt	1 teaspoonful sea salt
3 dessertspoonsful finely chopped fresh sage	6 teaspoonsful finely chopped fresh sage
3 cloves garlic	3 cloves garlic

1.   Cream the yeast and honey together and add the warm water. Leave the mixture in a warm place for 10 minutes or so until the yeast starts to work.

2.   In a large mixing bowl combine the flour, salt and finely chopped sage leaves. Crush the garlic cloves in a garlic press and add them to the flour, mixing well.

3.   Make a well in the centre of the flour and pour the yeast liquid into it. Mix it in well with a fork, then use the hands to press the mixture until it knits together in a soft dough.

4.   Turn the dough out onto a board, lightly sprinkle it with wholemeal flour and then knead it vigorously for about 10 to 15 minutes, then put it back in the mixing bowl and cover it with a clean cloth. Place the dough somewhere warm and leave it to rise until it has doubled in bulk.

5.   Turn the dough out again and sprinkle it with a little extra wholemeal flour. Continue to knead it for another couple of minutes until it feels soft and pliable again, adding more flour as necessary.

6.   Roll out the dough into a long sausage shape, about 16 inches (40cm) long. Place it on a well-oiled, flat baking tray and curve it around in a circle. Join the two ends together to form a ring and set it in the warmth again to rise for another 15 minutes or until it has doubled in size.

7.   Bake at 400°F/200°C (Gas Mark 6) for 15 minutes.

Note: For the best results, serve it hot, straight from the oven, with butter.

Illustrated opposite page 161.

Red Pepper and Onion Loaf

Makes 1 large loaf

Imperial/Metric American

Imperial/Metric	American
3 oz (85g) red pepper	3 ounces red pepper
4 oz (115g) onion	⅔ cupful onion
1¼ lb (565g) wholemeal flour	5 cupsful wholewheat flour
3 teaspoonsful sea salt	3 teaspoonsful sea salt
1 teaspoonful paprika pepper	1 teaspoonful paprika pepper
2 oz (55g) fresh yeast	¼ cupful fresh yeast
1 dessertspoonful honey	2 teaspoonsful honey
½ pint (285ml) warm water	1⅓ cupsful warm water

1. Chop the red pepper and the onion as finely as you can and place them in a large mixing bowl. Add the flour, salt and paprika pepper and mix them well together.

2. Blend the yeast, honey and warm water together in a small bowl and leave the mixture in a warm place until it starts to bubble.

3. Add the yeast mixture to the flour and blend the two sets of ingredients with a fork, then mix with the hands until the dough is formed.

4. Knead the dough vigorously on a floured surface for about 10 minutes, then put it back in the bowl, cover it with a cloth and leave it in a warm place until it has risen to twice its original size.

5. Knead the dough again for another few minutes. Shape the loaf and place it in a well-oiled 2 lb (1 kg) baking tin, then leave it to rise again for another 15-30 minutes until it reaches the top of the tin.

6. Bake at 400°F/200°C (Gas Mark 6) for 10 minutes, then reduce the heat to 350°F/180°C (Gas Mark 4) and bake for a further 40-45 minutes.

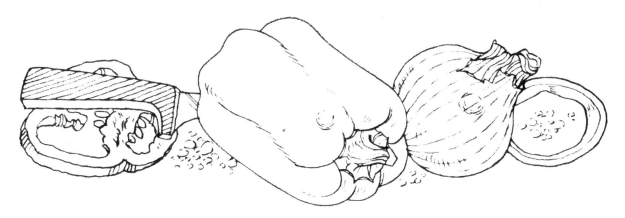

Bread Sticks

These can be served with soups or pâtés, put on the table instead of bread, or eaten as a between-meal snack.

Imperial/Metric	*American*
½ oz (15g) dried yeast	1 tablespoonful dried yeast
Approx. ⅓ pint (200ml) warm water	¾ cupful warm water
1 teaspoonful sea salt	1 teaspoonful sea salt
10 oz (285g) plain wholemeal flour	2½ cupsful plain wholewheat flour
Egg and milk to glaze	Egg and milk to glaze
Coarse sea salt	Coarse sea salt

1. Mix the yeast in a little of the warm water, and set aside.

2. Sift together the salt and flour, then stir in the bubbly yeast mixture and enough warm water to make a soft dough.

3. On a lightly floured board knead the dough for 5 minutes, until smooth and pliable. Place it in a warmed bowl, cover, and leave in a warm place for 1-2 hours, or until doubled in size.

4. Knead briefly again, return the dough to the bowl and set aside in the warm to rise again.

5. Now use a rolling pin to gently flatten pieces of the dough into rectangles about ¼ in. (6mm) thick.

6. Use a floured knife to cut these into 1 in. (2.5cm) wide strips, and use your hands to roll them into pencil-like sticks.

7. Arrange these, leaving a little space between them, on greased baking sheets and brush with a drop of egg and milk, beaten together.

8. Leave in the warm for a further hour to double in size. Brush lightly with more egg and milk, and sprinkle with coarse sea salt.

9. Bake at 400°F/200°C (Gas Mark 6) for 15-20 minutes, or until crisp. Cool on a wire rack and store in an airtight tin to use as needed.

Illustrated opposite page 96.

Desserts with a Difference

No-Cooking Lemon Soufflé

Imperial/Metric	American
1 packet agar-agar lemon jelly	1 packet agar-agar lemon jello
Grated rind and juice of a lemon	Grated rind and juice of a lemon
1 egg	1 egg
¼ pint (140ml) whipping cream	⅔ cupful whipping cream
1 orange	1 orange

1. Make up the jelly using just under ¾ pint/425ml (2 cupsful) of liquid (the lemon juice plus water).

2. Separate the egg and whisk the yolk into the jelly mixture, add the grated rind, and set aside to cool.

3. When it begins to firm up, stir in the stiffly beaten egg white and whipped cream, pour into a soufflé dish, and leave to set completely.

4. Decorate with orange slices before serving.

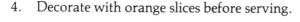

Crêpes Belle Hélène

For batter:

Imperial/Metric	American
4 oz (115g) plain wholemeal flour	1 cupful plain wholewheat flour
Pinch of sea salt	Pinch of sea salt
1 egg	1 egg
½ pint (285ml) milk, *or* half milk and half water	1⅓ cupsful milk, *or* half milk and half water

For filling:

Imperial/Metric	American
4 medium pears (Conference are ideal)	4 medium pears (Conference are ideal)
2 oz (55g) light Muscovado raw cane sugar	⅓ cupful light Muscovado raw cane sugar
A squeeze of lemon juice	A squeeze of lemon juice
1 teaspoonful grated lemon rind	1 teaspoonful grated lemon rind
2 oz (55g) bar raw sugar chocolate	2 ounce bar raw sugar chocolate
2 tablespoonsful milk *or* single cream	2 tablespoonsful milk *or* light cream
1 oz (30g) flaked almonds	¼ cupful slivered almonds

1. Sieve together the flour and salt, then add the egg and stir briefly.

2. Gradually pour in the liquid, stirring continually to blend in the flour and remove lumps, and continue beating until you have a smooth, creamy batter. Leave in the fridge for at least 30 minutes, then beat again before using.

3. Peel, core and quarter the pears; put them in a saucepan, cover with water, add sugar, lemon juice and rind, and simmer gently until tender.

4. In a bowl, over a pan of water, melt the broken chocolate, stirring continually, and adding enough milk or cream to make a sauce-like consistency.

5. Make up the pancakes in the usual way; fill each one with a portion of the coarsely chopped pears and a little of the juice; fold and top with some sauce and a sprinkling of nuts.

Dried Fruit Salad

Serves 6

Imperial/Metric	American
4 oz (115g) dried apricots	¾ cupful dried apricots
4 oz (115g) prunes	¾ cupful prunes
4 oz (115g) seedless raisins	¾ cupful seedless raisins
4 oz (115g) figs	¾ cupful figs
4 oz (115g) dates	¾ cupful dates
4 oz (115g) almonds, blanched	¾ cupful almonds, blanched
4 oz (115g) raw cane sugar	⅔ cupful raw cane sugar
2 tablespoonsful rosewater	2 tablespoonsful rosewater
2 tablespoonsful pine kernels (optional)	2 tablespoonsful pine kernels (optional)

1.   Mix all the ingredients in a large bowl and cover with cold water. Allow to soak for 2 days.

2.   Serve, possibly with the addition of preserved ginger and kirsch, and with whipped cream, if you wish.

Illustrated opposite page 177.

Pasta Caramel

Imperial/Metric	American
2 oz (55g) light Muscovado raw cane sugar	⅓ cupful light Muscovado raw cane sugar
2 tablespoonsful water	2 tablespoonsful water
1 pint (570ml) milk	2½ cupsful milk
4 oz (115g) wholemeal macaroni	2 cupsful wholewheat macaroni
Knob of polyunsaturated margarine	Knob of polyunsaturated margarine

1.   Put the sugar into a saucepan with the water; heat gently, stirring continually, until the sugar dissolves; cook a little longer to form a brown caramel mixture.

2.   Add the milk and heat gently.

3.   Add the macaroni and the margarine; continue cooking until the pasta is tender and most of the liquid has been absorbed.

4.   If you prefer, this mixture can be transferred to an ovenproof dish and baked at 300°F/150°C (Gas Mark 2) for 30 minutes.

Sicilian Cake

For sponge:

Imperial/Metric	American
2 eggs	2 eggs
2 oz (55g) raw cane sugar, powdered in grinder	⅓ cupful raw cane sugar, powdered in grinder
Vanilla essence	Vanilla essence
2 oz (55g) self-raising wholemeal flour	½ cupful self-raising wholewheat flour

For filling:

Imperial/Metric	American
1 lb (455g) Ricotta *or* curd cheese	2 cupsful Ricotta *or* curd cheese
6 oz (170g) raw cane sugar, powdered in grinder	1 cupful raw cane sugar, powdered in grinder
3-4 tablespoonsful *Maraschino, Cointreau* or *Grand Marnier* liqueur	⅓ cupful *Maraschino, Cointreau* or *Grand Marnier* liqueur
1 oz (30g) pistachio nuts *or* almonds	¼ cupful pistachio nuts *or* almonds
3 oz (85g) candied peel	½ cupful candied peel
2 oz (55g) bitter chocolate	2 ounces bitter chocolate

1.   To make the sponge, whisk together the eggs and sugar until the mixture thickens. Stir in the vanilla essence.

2.   Sieve the flour to make sure there are no lumps, then fold it into the eggs and sugar. If the eggs are small and the mixture rather dry, add a tiny drop of hot water.

3.   Spoon into a small, lined and greased loaf tin, and bake at 350°F/180°C (Gas Mark 4) for 20-25 minutes, or until you can press a finger firmly on the top of the cake and leave no impression.

4.   Turn out carefully and stand on a wire rack to cool.

5.   Sieve the cheese, then beat it together with the sugar and liqueur. Chop the nuts, candied peel and chocolate into small pieces, and stir them into the mixture.

6.   When the sponge is cold, cut it crossways into three long oblong strips about ½ in. (1cm) thick. Lay the first one on a flat plate and spread it with half the cheese mixture. Top with another sponge slice, then the rest of the cheese. Add the final slice of sponge and press down firmly.

7.   Cover the cake with foil and chill well, for at least two hours; before serving cut into thick slices. It is best taken from the fridge just before it is needed.

Note: If you want your Sicilian Cake to look more impressive, you can decorate it in a number of ways. The simplest is to divide the ingredients for the filling into two before you add the nuts, peel and chocolate. Proceed as above with one-half of the cheese, and shortly before serving, use the second half to make an icing over the top and sides of the sponge block. This can be decorated with grated chocolate, glacé cherries, chopped peel, more nuts — whatever takes your fancy.

Alternatively, make a chocolate icing and cover the cake with this, decorating it with candied fruit slices and glacé cherries, or by piping extra chocolate icing into patterns on top of the cake.

Blinis

For blinis:

Imperial/Metric	American
2 oz (55g) buckwheat flour	½ cupful buckwheat flour
2 oz (55g) plain wholemeal flour	½ cupful plain wholewheat flour
2 eggs	2 eggs
¼ pint (140ml) milk	⅔ cupful milk
Pinch of sea salt	Pinch of sea salt
1 tablespoonful vegetable oil	1 tablespoonful vegetable oil

For filling:

Imperial/Metric	American
½ lb (225g) cottage cheese, Ricotta *or* cream cheese	1 cupful cottage cheese, Ricotta *or* cream cheese
2 oz (55g) powdered raw cane sugar, *or* to taste	⅓ cupful powdered raw cane sugar, *or* to taste
Few drops vanilla essence *or* lemon juice	Few drops vanilla essence *or* lemon juice

1.   Sieve together the two flours and the salt.

2.   Use a wooden spoon to beat the eggs and milk into the dry ingredients; combine thoroughly.

3.   Heat the minimum amount of oil in a heavy-based pan (or simply brush with oil); pour in a little of the batter and make a pancake (crêpe) in the usual way.

4.   Mash the cheese with the sugar and essence or juice; use the mixture to fill the pancakes (crêpes); serve with raw sugar jam if liked.

Note: In fact, the accepted way to serve blinis is to fry them gently in a little butter after they have been filled. They need to be handled with care so that they do not fall apart, or lose their filling — cooking them this way does, of course, boost the fat involved, but for special occasions is well worth the extra effort. Dust with powdered sugar.

Tofu Cream Pie

For pastry:

Imperial/Metric	American
½ lb (225g) wholemeal flour	2 cupsful wholewheat flour
Pinch of sea salt	Pinch of sea salt
¼ teaspoonful cinnamon	¼ teaspoonful cinnamon
2 tablespoonsful vegetable oil	2 tablespoonsful vegetable oil
1 tablespoonful water	1 tablespoonful water
1½ tablespoonsful honey	1½ tablespoonsful honey

For filling:

Imperial/Metric	American
1 lb (455g) tofu	2 cupsful tofu
4 tablespoonsful water	¼ cupful water
6 oz (170g) honey	¾ cupful honey
1 teaspoonful *or* a few drops pure vanilla essence	1 teaspoonful *or* a few drops pure vanilla essence
2½ tablespoonsful lemon juice	2½ tablespoonsful lemon juice
2 teaspoonsful grated lemon rind	2 teaspoonsful grated lemon rind
¼ teaspoonful sea salt	¼ teaspoonful sea salt

1. Combine the flour, salt and cinnamon, and work in the oil, water and honey.

2. Press the pastry into a pie dish and bake for 10 minutes at 350°F/180°C (Gas Mark 4).

3. Blend all the filling ingredients and pour the mixture into the prepared pastry case, and continue cooking for 1 hour.

Mincemeat and Apple Crumble

Serves 6

For the mincemeat:

Imperial/Metric	American
½ lb (225g) raisins	1⅓ cupsful raisins
1 lb (455g) sultanas	2⅔ cupsful golden seedless raisins
½ lb (225g) cooking apples	8 ounces cooking apples
½ lb (225g) Brazil nuts	1½ cupsful Brazil nuts
½ lb (225g) vegetable fat	1 cupful vegetable fat
1 lb (455g) currants	2⅔ cupsful currants
Grated peel and juice from 2 lemons	Grated peel and juice from 2 lemons
Grated peel and juice from 2 oranges	Grated peel and juice from 2 oranges
1 teaspoonful nutmeg	1 teaspoonful nutmeg
2 tablespoonsful brandy	2 tablespoonsful brandy

1. Mince the raisins and sultanas (golden seedless raisins).

2. Grate the apples, Brazil nuts and fat.

3. Combine all the ingredients and mix well.

4. Keep in the refrigerator until required.

For the crumble:

Imperial/Metric	American
1 lb (455g) apples, peeled and sliced	1 pound apples, peeled and sliced
½ lb (225g) mincemeat	8 ounces mincemeat
½ teaspoonful cinnamon powder	½ teaspoonful cinnamon powder
6 oz (170g) wholemeal flour	1½ cupsful wholewheat flour
4 oz (115g) polyunsaturated margarine	½ cupful polyunsaturated margarine
1 tablespoonful oatflakes (optional)	1 tablespoonful oatflakes (optional)

1. Slice the apples into a casserole dish and sprinkle with cinnamon.

2. Spread mincemeat evenly over the apples.

3. Mix the flour and margarine and spread over the mincemeat. Top with flaked oats if you wish.

4. Bake at 350°F/180°C (Gas Mark 4) for 30 minutes until brown.

Illustrated between pages 96 and 97.

Chocolate Mousse

Serves 6

Imperial/Metric	*American*
¾ lb (340g) plain raw sugar chocolate	¾ pound plain raw sugar chocolate
6 tablespoonsful black coffee	½ cupful black coffee
1 oz (30g) butter	2½ tablespoonsful butter
2 tablespoonsful rum	2 tablespoonsful rum
3 drops vanilla essence	3 drops vanilla essence
6 eggs, separated	6 eggs, separated
½ pint (285ml) double cream, whipped	1⅓ cupsful heavy cream, whipped

1. Break the chocolate into small pieces, put into a bowl with the coffee and place the bowl over a saucepan of boiling water. Stir to a thick cream.

2. Stir in the butter, rum and vanilla.

3. Remove the bowl from the heat and stir in the egg yolks. Mix well.

4. Whisk the egg whites until they are stiff.

5. Stir the beaten egg-whites into the chocolate.

6. Spoon the mousse into wine glasses and put into a cool place for several hours to set.

7. Pipe whipped cream generously onto the top of the individual mousses.

Illustrated opposite page 176.

Coeur à la Creme

Imperial/Metric	*American*
½ lb (225g) cream cheese	1 cupful cream cheese
⅛ pint (70ml) plain yogurt	¼ cupful plain yogurt
½ lb (225g) fresh raspberries *or* strawberries	8 ounces fresh raspberries *or* strawberries
2 oz (55g) raw cane sugar	⅓ cupful raw cane sugar

1. Blend the cheese and yogurt until smooth.

2. Pack into a mould (a heart shape is traditional); chill for at least 2-3 hours.

3. Tip from the mould onto a serving plate, garnish with the fruit and sprinkle with sugar.

Chilled Rice Pudding

Imperial/Metric	American
¾ pint (425ml) water	2 cupsful water
¾ pint (425ml) milk	2 cupsful milk
10 oz (285g) plain brown rice	1¼ cupsful plain brown rice
10 oz (285g) sweet brown rice*	1¼ cupsful sweet brown rice*
1 oz (30g) ground almonds	1¼ cupsful ground almonds
2 tablespoonsful apple concentrate	2 tablespoonsful apple concentrate
Skinned and roasted whole almonds	Skinned and roasted whole almonds

1. Mix water and milk and bring to the boil.

2. Mix the plain and sweet rice, then stir it into the liquid and cover.

3. Cook briskly for 12 minutes.

4. Meanwhile mix almonds and apple concentrate and add to the cooking rice.

5. Turn heat low and simmer for a further 30 minutes.

6. Place in individual dessert dishes and leave to cool. Decorate with whole almonds and chill before serving.

* Sweet brown rice is a very glutinous variety originating from Japan. Its sweet flavour and moist texture when cooked make it ideal for desserts where one wishes to keep sweeteners to a minimum.

Stuffed Apples

Imperial/Metric	American
2 oz (55g) wholemeal spaghetti rings	½ cupful wholewheat spaghetti rings
4 large apples	4 large apples
4 oz (115g) raw sugar mincemeat	⅓ cupful raw sugar mincemeat
2 oz (55g) chopped roasted hazelnuts	½ cupful chopped roasted hazelnuts
½ oz (15g) polyunsaturated margarine	1 tablespoonful polyunsaturated margarine
1 tablespoonful honey	1 tablespoonful honey
Squeeze of lemon juice	Squeeze of lemon juice
1 small carton plain yogurt (optional)	1 small carton plain yogurt (optional)
¼ pint (140ml) single cream (optional)	⅔ cupful light cream (optional)

1.   Cook the pasta in boiling water until tender; drain, then set aside.

2.   Wash, dry, and remove the centre cores from the apples; make a slit around the skins so that the apples do not burst in the oven.

3.   In a bowl, mix together the pasta, mincemeat, nuts and margarine. Stuff the apples with this mixture.

4.   Arrange the apples side by side in an ovenproof dish; mix the honey with the lemon juice and trickle over the top of the apples.

5.   Bake at 350°F/180°C (Gas Mark 4) for about 20 minutes, or until the apples are cooked.

6.   Serve hot or cold.

Note: Yogurt and single (light) cream whipped lightly together, then chilled, makes a fresh contrast to the sweetness of this dish.

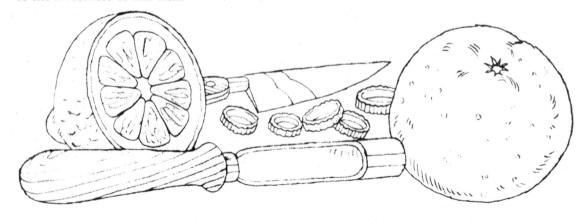

Melon Water Ice

Imperial/Metric	American
1 large ogen melon	1 large ogen melon
4 oz (115g) raw cane sugar	⅔ cupful raw cane sugar
¼ pint (140ml) water	⅔ cupful water
1 teaspoonful lemon juice	1 teaspoonful lemon juice
Stem ginger preserved in honey (optional)	Stem ginger preserved in honey (optional)

1.   Peel, seed, and coarsely chop the melon before puréeing the flesh in a blender, or pushing it through a sieve.

2.   Combine the sugar and water in a saucepan, heat gently and stir until the sugar dissolves. Raise the heat and boil the mixture for 4-5 minutes more, without stirring, then set aside to cool.

3.   Add the syrup to the melon purée, stir in the lemon juice, and pour the mixture into a shallow freezing tray. Set the freezer on a high setting, and leave the mixture until it begins to firm up. Whip lightly to add air and improve the texture. Re-freeze.

4.   Serve in chilled glasses. A few pieces of stem ginger, and a spoonful of the liquid in which they were preserved make a perfect topping.

Honeyed Fruit Flan

For pastry:

Imperial/Metric	American
4 oz (115g) polyunsaturated margarine	½ cupful polyunsaturated margarine
4 oz (115g) plain wholemeal flour	1 cupful plain wholewheat flour
1 tablespoonful honey	1 tablespoonful honey
Cold water to mix	Cold water to mix

For filling:

Imperial/Metric	American
½ lb (225g) dried apricot halves	1⅓ cupsful dried apricot halves
1 tablespoonful honey	1 tablespoonful honey
1 tablespoonful lemon juice	1 tablespoonful lemon juice
1 teaspoonful cinnamon	1 teaspoonful cinnamon
2 large bananas	2 large bananas
Approx. 20 firm green grapes	Approx. 20 firm green grapes

1.   Soak the apricots overnight.

2.   Make the pastry by rubbing the margarine into the flour to produce a fine breadcrumb mixture, then binding with enough water to make a firm dough.

3.   Knead in the honey, then wrap in aluminium foil or clingfilm and chill for 30 minutes.

4.   Roll out the pastry and use to line a small flan dish; prick the bottom with a fork, then bake 'blind' at 350°F/180°C (Gas Mark 4) for about 20 minutes, or until crisp.

5.   Combine honey and lemon juice, add cinnamon, then stir in the drained plumped apricot halves, the bananas cut into chunks, and the grapes. It is important that each piece of fruit is coated in the honey syrup — you may need to make up a little more.

6.   When pastry case has cooled, arrange the fruit in decorative circles. Any extra syrup can be poured over the top, and for a spicier taste, a final sprinkling of cinnamon can be added.

Illustrated opposite page 144.

Opposite: The finishing touch to a perfect dinner party — a selection of light, refreshing desserts. Chocolate Mousse (page 172), Lemon Yogurt (page 182) and Tofu Maple Fruit Whip (page 182).

Crêpes with Pineapple and Ginger

For batter:

Imperial/Metric	American
4 oz (115g) plain wholemeal flour	1 cupful plain wholewheat flour
Pinch of sea salt	Pinch of sea salt
2 large eggs	2 large eggs
½ pint (285ml) milk	1⅓ cupsful milk

For filling:

Imperial/Metric	American
1 small pineapple *or* 1 tin of pineapple in natural juice	1 small pineapple *or* 1 can of pineapple in natural juice
A few pieces of stem ginger preserved in honey	A few pieces of stem ginger preserved in honey
4 oz (115g) wholemeal ginger biscuits	4 ounces wholewheat ginger biscuits

1.   Sieve together the flour and salt, then add the eggs and stir briefly.

2.   Gradually pour in the liquid, stirring continually to blend in the flour and remove lumps, and continue beating until you have a smooth creamy batter. Leave in the fridge for at least 30 minutes, then beat again before using.

3.   Crush the pineapple flesh (not too fine or it will disintegrate) and moisten with some of the natural juice and/or a few spoonsful of the ginger-flavoured honey; mix in the finely chopped ginger. Crumble the biscuits coarsely and mix half of them with the fruit.

4.   Make up the pancakes in the usual way; fill each one with some of the fruit mixture; fold and sprinkle with the remaining ginger crumbs.

Note: You could also make a sauce by heating together 2 oz/55g (⅓ cupful) light Muscovado raw cane sugar with about ½ pint/285ml (1⅓ cupsful) pineapple juice and ginger honey combined, and stirring until the sauce thickens. Serve over the pancakes (crêpes) and then sprinkle with crumbs, if desired.

Opposite: Dried Fruit Salad (page 167) rounds of an exotic Middle Eastern meal of Lentils and Spinach (page 60) with Pitta Bread (page 86).

Cheesecake

For pastry:

Imperial/Metric	American
½ lb (225g) plain wholemeal flour	2 cupsful plain wholewheat flour
Pinch of salt	Pinch of salt
6 oz (170g) polyunsaturated margarine *or* butter	¾ cupful polyunsaturated margarine *or* butter
2 egg yolks	2 egg yolks
1 teaspoonful grated lemon peel	1 teaspoonful grated lemon peel
Cold water to mix	Cold water to mix

For filling:

Imperial/Metric	American
1 lb (455g) Ricotta cheese	1 cupful Ricotta cheese
1 oz (30g) plain wholemeal flour	¼ cupful plain wholewheat flour
1 tablespoonful grated orange peel	1 tablespoonful grated orange peel
2 tablespoonsful sultanas	2 tablespoonsful golden seedless raisins
Vanilla essence	Vanilla essence
4 oz (115g) raw cane sugar, powdered in grinder	⅔ cupful raw cane sugar, powdered in grinder
3 eggs	3 eggs
1 oz (30g) flaked almonds	¼ cupful slivered almonds

1.   Sift together the flour and salt, then rub in the margarine to make a breadcrumb-like mixture.

2.   Beat the egg yolks lightly and mix into the flour and margarine, sprinkle in the lemon peel, and add just enough cold water to bind the ingredients together. Knead briefly then cover and chill.

3.   Combine the cheese and sifted flour, blending them well so that the mixture is smooth. Stir in the grated peel, sultanas (golden seedless raisins), a drop of vanilla essence, and lastly the sugar.

4.   Beat the eggs until they begin to foam, and stir into the other ingredients.

5.   Roll out the pastry and use to line an 8 in. (20cm) loose-bottomed flan dish, or ring standing on a baking sheet. Pour in the filling, spreading it evenly and then scatter the flaked (slivered) almonds over the top. (Any extra pastry can be used to make a decorative lattice pattern.)

6.   Bake at 350°F/180°C (Gas Mark 4) for 50 minutes to 1 hour, or until the filling is firm and the pastry cooked. Cool slightly, then transfer carefully to a wire rack and leave to get completely cold. This rich cheesecake is especially good served with a fresh fruit such as white grapes.

Note: If you cannot obtain Ricotta cheese, try this recipe using curd cheese, or sieved cottage cheese with a few spoonsful of cream added. And those with a sweeter tooth might prefer using chopped, candied peel in the filling rather than the sharper tasting fresh orange and lemon.

Rice and Carrot Pudding

If you wish, substitute an equal weight of cooked pumpkin for the carrots.

Imperial/Metric	American
1 lb (455g) carrots, cooked	2½ cupsful cooked carrots
7 oz (200g) cooked short-grain brown rice	1¼ cupsful cooked short-grain brown rice
2 fl oz (60ml) fresh apple juice	¼ cupful fresh apple juice
1 tablespoonful apple juice concentrate, barley-malt syrup *or* rice syrup	1 tablespoonful apple juice concentrate, barley-malt syrup *or* rice syrup
2 tablespoonsful hot vegetable oil	2 tablespoonsful hot vegetable oil
Pinch each of nutmeg, cinnamon and grated ginger	Pinch each of nutmeg, cinnamon and grated ginger
1 beaten egg	1 beaten egg
3 oz (85g) currants *or* raisins	½ cupful currants *or* raisins

1.   Purée carrots and add all ingredients. Mix thoroughly, adding more apple juice if needed.

2.   Bake in an oiled baking dish at 350°F/180°C (Gas Mark 4) for 30-40 minutes. (Place the baking dish in a larger pan with 1 in./2.5cm depth of water to prevent scorching when in the oven.)

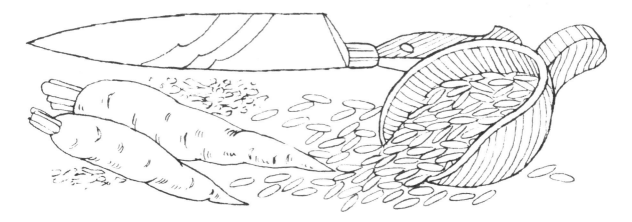

Srikand

Serves 6

Imperial/Metric	American
2 pints (1 litre) plain yogurt	5 cupsful plain yogurt
8 white cardamoms	8 white cardamoms
A pinch of saffron	A pinch of saffron
1 tablespoonful rosewater	1 tablespoonful rosewater
4 oz (115g) raw cane sugar	⅔ cupful raw cane sugar
2 tablespoonsful cashews, coarsely chopped	2 tablespoonsful cashews, coarsely chopped
2 tablespoonsful raisins, coarsely chopped	2 tablespoonsful raisins, coarsely chopped

1.   Put the yogurt in a muslin bag and allow to drain overnight. The solid residue is similar to curd cheese and curd cheese could be used instead of the yogurt if you do not wish to make it yourself.

2.   Remove the black seeds from the centre of the cardamoms and discard the husks. Crush the seeds or grind them in your spice grinder.

3.   Dissolve the saffron in the rosewater.

4.   Combine all the ingredients and mix well.

5.   Place in a refrigerator to chill.

6.   Serve garnished possibly with a maraschino cherry or a few chopped pistachios.

Creamy Coconut Pizza

For base:

Imperial/Metric	American
½ teaspoonful dried yeast	½ teaspoonful dried yeast
¼ pint (140ml) warm water	⅔ cupful warm water
1 tablespoonful vegetable oil	1 tablespoonful vegetable oil
½ lb (225g) plain wholemeal flour	2 cupsful plain wholewheat flour

For topping:

Imperial/Metric	American
2 oz (55g) polyunsaturated margarine	¼ cupful polyunsaturated margarine
2 oz (55g) light Muscovado raw cane sugar	⅓ cupful light Muscovado raw cane sugar
3 oz (85g) desiccated coconut	1 cupful desiccated coconut
3 tablespoonsful double cream *or* sieved cottage cheese *or* cream cheese	3 tablespoonsful heavy cream *or* sieved cottage cheese *or* cream cheese

1.   Sprinkle the yeast onto the warm water, stir, and set aside until the mixture bubbles. Stir in the oil, then gradually add the liquid to the sifted flour.

2.   When this becomes difficult, turn the dough onto a floured board and knead for 5-10 minutes to make a soft, elastic dough.

3.   Shape dough into circles or use to line a Swiss-roll tin; bake at 400°F/200°C (Gas Mark 6) for 20-30 minutes.

4.   In a bowl mix together the margarine, sugar and coconut; add the cream and blend thoroughly.

5.   When the pizza base is cooked, spread the mixture over it evenly and put under a grill for just a few minutes until the topping is golden and bubbly. Serve immediately as a dessert, or — if baking in a Swiss-roll tin — cut into slices, allow to cool, and serve as a cake.

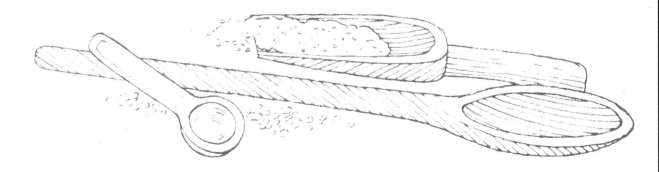

181

Lemon Yogurts

Imperial/Metric	American
1 pint (570ml) plain yogurt	2½ cupsful plain yogurt
4 good tablespoonsful raw sugar lemon curd	⅓ cupful raw sugar lemon curd
Raw sugar chocolate (optional)	Raw sugar chocolate (optional)

1. Stir the lemon curd into the yogurt and mix thoroughly. Chill for an hour if possible before serving.

2. Divide between four glasses or dishes, and top with a little flaked (slivered) chocolate.

Illustrated opposite page 176.

Tofu Maple Fruit Whip

Imperial/Metric	American
½ lb (225g) tofu	1⅓ cupsful tofu
½ lb (225g) ripe fresh fruit, such as apricots, pear, blackcurrants, etc.	2 cupsful ripe fresh fruit, such as apricots, pear, blackcurrants, etc.
Maple syrup to taste	Maple syrup to taste
A few nuts	A few nuts

1. Just combine the first three ingredients and blend them until thick and creamy. (This is best done in a blender, but can also be done by hand.)

2. Spoon the mixture into two or three small dishes, and chill.

3. Sprinkle some chopped nuts over the top if desired.

Illustrated opposite page 176.

Banana Walnut Crêpes (Vegan)

For batter:

Imperial/Metric	American
4 oz (115g) plain wholemeal flour	1 cupful plain wholewheat flour
2 oz (55g) soya flour	½ cupful soy flour
1 teaspoonful baking powder	1 teaspoonful baking powder
½ pint (285ml) water	1⅓ cupsful water
Pinch of sea salt	Pinch of sea salt

For filling:

Imperial/Metric	American
4 ripe bananas	4 ripe bananas
A squeeze of lemon juice	A squeeze of lemon juice
2 tablespoonsful maple syrup	2 tablespoonsful maple syrup
2 oz (55g) walnut pieces	½ cupful English walnut pieces
1 oz (30g) vegan margarine	2½ tablespoonsful vegan margarine

1.   Sieve together the flours, baking powder and salt. Gradually stir in the water, then beat for a few minutes.

2.   Leave in the fridge for at least 30 minutes, then beat again before using.

3.   Mash the bananas to a smooth cream with the lemon juice and syrup; gently sauté the walnut pieces in the melted fat.

4.   Make up the pancakes (crêpes) and fill each one with the banana cream; fold and sprinkle with the nuts before serving.

Note: As an alternative you can cut the banana into chunks, toss in the combined juice and syrup, and mix with the raw coarsely chopped nuts. Use a little melted margarine instead of a sauce to trickle over the top of your folded pancakes (crêpes).

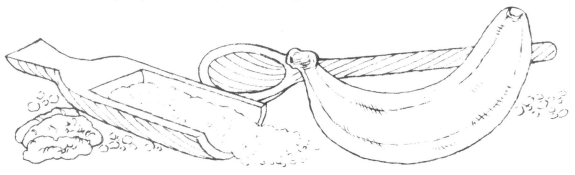

Semolina with Fruit and Nuts

Imperial/Metric	American
3 oz (85g) polyunsaturated margarine	⅓ cupful polyunsaturated margarine
2 oz (55g) raisins	2 tablespoonsful raisins
1 oz (30g) almonds *or* walnuts	¼ cupful almonds *or* English walnuts
4 oz (115g) raw cane sugar	⅔ cupful raw cane sugar
4 oz (115g) wholemeal semolina	1 cupful wholewheat semolina
⅔ pint (340ml) milk	1½ cupsful milk

1. Heat 1 oz (30g) of the margarine and gently fry the raisins and chopped nuts for a few minutes, then set aside.

2. Melt the rest of the margarine, add the sugar and semolina and cook for a few minutes more; then pour in the milk very slowly, stirring continually.

3. Cook gently, still stirring, until the mixture thickens and the semolina is ready.

4. Pour into bowls that have been rinsed in cold water, leave to cool; top with the fruit and nuts before serving.

Mango Fool

Serves 6

Imperial/Metric *American*

4 oz (115g) creamed coconut	4 ounces creamed coconut
8 white cardamom seeds	8 white cardamom seeds
1 large tin mango purée	1 large can mango paste
1 tablespoonful lemon juice	1 tablespoonful lemon juice
½ pint (285ml) double cream, whisked	1⅓ cupsful heavy cream, whisked

1. Put a little water in a saucepan and, over a gentle heat, melt the creamed coconut.

2. Remove the black seeds from the centre of the cardamoms and discard the husks.

3. Combine the mango purée, coconut, lemon juice and cardamom seeds.

4. Spoon into wineglasses and allow to stand in the refrigerator for an hour or so.

5. Pipe cream round the edges of the glass or whirl it into the mango to create a whirl of white in the orange colouring.

Egg Custard Surprises

Imperial/Metric	American
4 oz (115g) wholemeal spaghetti rings	2 cupsful wholewheat spaghetti rings
2 oz (55g) raisins	2 tablespoonsful raisins
2 oz (55g) candied peel	2 tablespoonsful candied peel
2 or 3 eggs	2 or 3 eggs
1 pint (570ml) milk	2½ cupsful milk
1 oz (30g) raw cane sugar	2 tablespoonsful raw cane sugar
Grated nutmeg	Grated nutmeg

1. Cook the spaghetti rings in water (or milk) until just tender; drain well and divide between 4 small soufflé or ovenproof dishes.

2. Sprinkle each one with some of the raisins and chopped peel.

3. In a bowl, whisk together the eggs and warmed milk; add the sugar; pour over the pasta and fruit, preferably through a strainer; sprinkle with nutmeg.

4. Stand the dishes in a tin of hot water and bake at 325°F/170°C (Gas Mark 3) for 1 hour, or until set.

Almond Orange Ambrosia

Imperial/Metric	American
4 oranges	4 oranges
4 oz (115g) sliced almonds, raw *or* roasted	1 cupful sliced almonds, raw *or* roasted
2-4 oz (55-115g) raw cane sugar	⅓-⅔ cupful raw cane sugar
Pure orange juice	Pure orange juice

1.   Slice the oranges finely and arrange in layers, alternating with the nuts and half of the sugar, in one attractive serving dish, or four smaller bowls.

2.   Sprinkle the remaining sugar over the top and pour on enough orange juice to moisten the fruit. Cover and chill, preferably overnight.

Pecan Pie

Imperial/Metric	American
Pastry to line an 8 in. (20cm) flan dish (see page 61)	Pastry to line an 8 inch flan dish (see page 61)
½ lb (225g) molasses raw cane sugar	1⅓ cupsful molasses raw cane sugar
½ lb (225g) honey *or* syrup	⅔ cupful honey *or* syrup
2 oz (55g) polyunsaturated margarine	¼ cupful polyunsaturated margarine
3 eggs	3 eggs
5 oz (140g) halved pecan nuts	1 cupful halved pecan nuts

1. Carefully line the flan dish with the pastry and set aside.

2. Mix together the sugar, honey and melted margarine.

3. Beat the eggs, then add to the sugar mixture, and combine thoroughly.

4. Stir in the pecans.

5. Pour the filling into the flan dish and bake at 400°F/200°C (Gas Mark 6) for 10 minutes, then at 350°F/180°C (Gas Mark 4) for about 30 minutes more, or until the filling has set.

6. Serve warm (not hot), or let cool completely.

Note: Walnuts (English walnuts) can be used in place of the pecans, if desired.

Index